FAIR HAVEN BR
182 GRAND AVENUE
NEW HAVEN, CT 06513

SO-EHZ-963

HOW TO GET A JOB IN THE USA

A Step-by-Step Guide for Immigrants, Foreign Nationals
and Anyone Entering or Re-entering the US Job Market
(Emphasizing American Business Communication Basics)

FAIR HAVEN LIBRARY
182 GRAND AVENUE
NEW HAVEN CT 06513

Nara Venditti, Ph.D.

www.SucceedinAmerica.com

Succeed in America Books

HOW TO GET A JOB IN THE USA

A Step-by-Step Guide for Immigrants, Foreign Nationals and Anyone Entering or Re-entering the US Job Market

(Emphasizing American Business Communication Basics)

ISBN 0-9777054-0-4

A Succeed in America™ Book

Copyright © 2006 by Nara Venditti, Ph.D.

All rights reserved including the right to translate and reproduce this book or any portion thereof in ﹍ y form. Request for such permissions should be addressed to Succeed in America, LLC.

Published by *Succeed in America, LLC*
P.O. Box 4724
Danbury, CT 06813-4724, USA
(203) 791-1107
www.SucceedinAmerica.com

Special discounts on bulk quantities of Succeed in America books are available.

For information and future updates, visit the Succeed in America website: www.SucceedinAmerica.c ﹍ ﹍

 A Succeed in America ™ Series and logo and the title and trade dress are the intellectual property of Succeed in America, LLC.

Library of Congress Control Number 2005911312
ISBN 0-9777054-0-4

First Edition
Printed in Canada

DISCLAIMER

Neither **Succeed in America™** nor the authors are responsible for errors in or omissions of information regardi ﹍ ﹍ any organizations or websites referenced or listed here or elsewhere on succeedinamerica.com. All sources listed are those the author have personally used and prefer but are not the only ones available. The accuracy of information is not guaranteed as laws and regulations and website addresses may change or be subject to differing interpretations.

Any actions taken based on information from books or resources listed here are taken solely at the discretion of the individual and are in no way the responsibility of **Succeed in America™** or its employees.

Here's what others are saying about the book and seminars:

Dear Dr. Venditti,
Almost two months ago I attended one of your seminars. After following all the steps you taught me, I applied for the job of my dreams and for my surprise they called me and I got it!!! First I thank God and I also thank you for everything you taught us that day!
Norma Santos, U.S. permanent resident, native of Brazil

Our ESL clients enjoyed and learned a great deal from Nara's "How To Get A Job In The USA" program here at Danbury Library. Her sound advice and tips on the American job hunting culture should be helpful to anyone seeking employment in the United States.
Elissa, Scudder, ESL Coordinator, Danbury Public Library, Connecticut, USA

Nara,
Just a quick note to tell you that I got a hotel job!!! I had read and studied some parts of your CD and presentation before the interview and was well prepared. Thank you soooo much for you help! Take care and once again, thank you for your help in making this happen!
Gabriel Mayor Gavier, hotel industry professional, native of Argentina

On behalf of Greenwich Library, I would like to thank you so much for your very informative workshop, How to Get a Job in the USA... You facilitated a very diverse group effectively. Your workshop stressed the benefit of networking and it was interesting to note that was precisely what the participants seemed to enjoy: networking with each other! The stated goals of many at the workshop were to learn to speak English better and to get better jobs in the USA. Your concern for helping them to achieve their goals was evident. The coaching you gave them Sunday afternoon should help them to achieve their version of the American Dream!
Wynne Delmhorst, Adult Programs Coordinator, Greenwich, CT Library, USA

When in Rome, do as the Romans. The company that hires not only looks for a skillful candidates but one who fits in. This book is an excellent guide on the job or interview search and how it is conducted in the US. Knowing what you can expect should make you more relaxed and enables you to sell your talent more effectively.
Mauri A. Korhonen, Vice President and General Manager,
Ingenico Customer Services, US and Canada, native of Finland

The workshop was informative, intense, and also very practical. Patrons, who attended the workshop were interacting in groups, and participated in role play trainings. They had very comprehensive handouts. I think this workshop could be very useful not only for people, who are immigrants in the USA and have a different cultural, educational and language background, but for everyone who is trying to get successfully through the career change or refresh the knowledge and experience of going through job hunting and interview process.

Yelena Klompus, World Languages & Literacy Librarian,
Ferguson Library, Stamford, CT, USA

Dedication

To my Dad, who always encouraged and inspired me to be my best, and to work hard for success. My Dad was the only one in our family who never made it to this country. Trapped by a terrible disease and hardship, he gave me his blessing to start a new life in America. He passed away as I was flying into New York City.

To my Mom, who came to this country in her golden years. With the same passion and determination that she used to overcome all the obstacles in her life, she conquered the English language and passed her citizenship exam with flying colors. She embraced new life and new technology and is an avid user of the Internet.

To my Daughter, who does not realize that she is the incarnation of my American dream. There is nothing in the world more precious than you!

To Robert Hart Aldrich, my first American mentor, for unveiling the mysteries of the American culture in my initial quest for employment in the USA.

Acknowledgements

This book is the product of the experiences, knowledge and opinions of many who gave their time, energy and encouragement during the writing of this book.

To my book consultant,

First and foremost, thank you Robyn Whittingham. Many authors thank their consultants. My consultant is special. As a human resource professional and a recruiter hiring for the global workforce on a daily basis, she validated my idea to write this book. She is an American who came to understand about cultures through her work and personal contact with non-American-born professionals, including me. Her all-American positive attitude and tremendous support and advice throughout the work made it all possible.

To the authors of the books on job search and self-improvement,

Although your help was not through personal contact, reading your books gave me valuable insight into the job search process and culture in this country. As a result, I have cited your books at the end of applicable sections/chapters of my book as recommended further reading.

To human resource professionals·and hiring managers,

This book was enhanced numerous times by your advice and feedback. As a member of Western Connecticut Society for Human Resource Management (SHRM), I know what kinds of challenges you have to deal with every day, and I appreciate the time you took to look over my manuscript and provide suggestions for improvement.

To job seekers and workshop participants,

Your wonderful comments on my book and seminars have been and continue to be a source of great satisfaction and inspiration for me. To successful job seekers including Manish Shah, Norma Santos, Gabriel Gavier, Kristina Muradian, Vyacheslav Pradkin, Said Ismail, Sonia de Sa, John Chang, all the members of Diversity-USA Toastmasters Club of Danbury, CT and many, many others. Your success is my success. Good luck to you all!

To Toastmasters International,

Thanks to *Toastmasters International, an* organization which helps individuals throughout the world become better communicators and leaders. As a member I was presented opportunities I never dreamed of, including a network of people whose friendship and support transformed my life.

My profound thanks to Richard Hastings, Esq., DTM, and Edina Soboleski, DTM, for their invaluable support and advice.

Also, special thanks to Guidance Committee members of the *High Performance Leadership Program* for their advice on the contents of *How to Get a Job in the USA.* Thank you to Cynthia Slater, Bob Lenz, Gail Palermo, Pat Kelly, Edina Soboleski, for reading the first drafts of the book. Special thanks to Richard Hastings for his continuous advice and guidance on how to bring the book to market and reading segments of the book.

Thank you, District 53 clubs, Diversity-USA and Wooster Heights Toastmasters, for your supportive feedback on my presentations of the book content.

To subject matter experts,

Thanks to Myra Oliver, the Executive Director of International Institute of Connecticut, for reading excerpts and invaluable advice on Chapter 1, *Who can work in the US?*

James Frey, Ed.D., President, Educational Credentials Evaluators, Inc. and Bonnie Rosenthal of Evaluation Service, Inc. for advice on credential evaluation (Chapter 2, *Educational Credentials*).

I deeply appreciate Linda Fein for her valuable comments on the final versions as well as: LouAnn Bloomer, Jo Gabriel and Mary Cipriano of TBICO, Dr. Walter Bernstein, VP for Student Affairs, and Dr. Walter Cramer, Dean of Student Affairs, Western Connecticut State University (WSCU), Prof. Fred Tesch of Ancell School of Business, WCSU, Directors Maureen Casey Gernert, Anthony Ciarleglio and Asst. Director Lisa Temkin Carrozza of WCSU Career Development Center; Riall Nolan, Dean of International Programs at Purdue University; Diane Steeves, Manager, Dutchess, Danbury, CT, Alfred J. Mariani, President, Résumés Etc., Fred Rhines, President, Remedy Staffing, Diane Mull, Regional Director for Community Outreach, Money Management International, Sheryle L. McMillan, Community Development Banking, Bank of America, John La Cava, Esq. of Barr & LaCava, Nancy Haas, President, WC SHRM, for her comments on Chapter 4, Kelly Garretson, SPHR, for commenting on legal aspects of interviewing and many other subject matter experts for their comments and support.

To Cendant Mobility,

Where I had the opportunity to take a good look at the American workplace culture in action and to understand what American employers are looking for in their employees.

My very special thanks to Patrice Heinzer – for reading segments of my book and for invaluable advice and support. Bill Maxwell for reading segments of the book, the table of contents and for validating the book idea. Trey Delmark, Janis Leet, Robert Sanford, Hamilton Farias, Andrea Scalici, Vasu Anburajan – for giving feedback on what American employers are looking for in their new hires. Tom Davis and Dyanne Calder for marketing advice. To all of the leadership and my associates at Cendant, especially members of Emerging Markets team.

To my book designers and copy editors,

Thank you, Russell Stockton for your book and cover design. I sincerely appreciate your patience, diligence and talent which greatly contributed to the appearance of my book!

Thank you, Lisa Zielinski of Hignell Book Printing for finalizing the cover.

Thank you Liz Abraham, a connoisseur of American English, for straightening out my "accented writing" in the first pass editing of Chapter 1 to 7. Thank you, Ronnie Backer for initial readings of the Prologue and Chapter 1.

Thank you Phil Sarnik, who graciously agreed to edit the final versions of the book.

To friends and family,

To Rick, who was very patient with my project and read the first version of the manuscript as well as many segments in the final version.

To all my friends whose enthusiasm fueled my commitment to the project.

To my daughter Elena, to my mother Karina, to my son-in-law Mike and step dad Eddie for their support and love.

There is no way I can list everybody and express gratitude to all of you.

FOREWORD

In the few years of writing this book, I have read scores of books and talked to hundreds of job seekers, hiring managers and human resource professionals who have educated me on the subject of the American job market. They have enlightened me on their desires and needs, as well as the challenges they have faced in achieving their respective goals. While it is my hope that I have addressed the majority of their concerns in this book, I will use my website www.SucceedinAmerica.com and Succeed in America Newsletter as resources for posting updated information on the ever-changing world of the American workplace.

TABLE OF CONTENTS

Prologue

On the Way to Success in America

Olga Petrovskaya did not understand why it took so long for her to get a job in America. She had graduated from the top technical school in Ukraine, Kharkiv Polytechnic, with honors. She had been the most valuable IT manager in a very successful Ukrainian jewelry manufacturing plant for the past two years. When her family moved to the US, she was not worried at all about the transition. Her English, she thought, was fairly good and her profession was in great demand in America.

But things did not go as smoothly as she had anticipated. Potential employers were impressed with her credentials as well as her resume, which she had created with the help of an American friend. However, although she went to many interviews, she did not receive any job offers.

She could not understand why. In her mind she replayed again and again her most recent interview. Yes, she wore her best dress, the one with a little lace collar and buttons down the back; it went perfectly well with her new red patent leather shoes with silver buckles. She recalled that the recruiter, a man, seemed somewhat strange to her: he extended his hand for a handshake first. How rude, thought Olga. Shouldn't he wait until she, a woman, extended hers first? Then he had smiled at her throughout the interview. Did that mean he fancied her? She tried to avoid his eyes and maintain a very somber expression so that he did not get any ideas. Instead of asking for documents —such as her diploma, which she had translated and notarized —he asked strange questions like," Tell me about a time when you had to think out of the box." Do they put you into a box so that you can think better? Olga wondered. She did not understand some of the questions, but was too shy to ask him what he meant. During the interview she became so stressed that she had to light a cigarette to relax. But these incidents seemed minor to her. After all, he kept smiling, didn't he? At one point, however, she acknowledged, he had stopped his smiling and friendly manners. Was it when she asked about the salary and vacation days?

Can you guess why Olga did not get the job offer? What went wrong? The fact is, despite her best efforts, she did almost **everything** wrong. And probably somebody else with similar credentials —but who was knowledgeable about American interviewing culture and how to handle the interview process —got the job.

What do *you* think of Olga's interview experience? I invite you to identify the behaviors that kept Olga from being offered a job for which she was well qualified.

Olga's Mistakes

Listed below are reasons Olga's interview performance was diminished. In the right hand column, write what you think Olga should have done or said.

What Olga Did Wrong Or Did Not Know	What Olga Should Have Done Or Said
Was dressed inappropriately	_____
Did not maintain eye contact	_____
Misinterpreted her interviewer's smile	_____
Did not understand a phrase	_____
Lit a cigarette	_____

After you have read this book and completed the worksheets provided, re-read the examples above, and review your list. See how your perception of Olga's behavior has changed, and how much you've learned! This book will give you the information and insight you need to find a job in the United States of America.

Introduction

Why This Book Was Written and For Whom

This book is about the American job search culture. It is a guide that will help turn you into a successful job seeker.

Every year millions of people come to the United States. They come for many reasons: to study, to build a new life, to join another family member on a corporate assignment, or to escape an oppressive regime. No matter what your reason for coming, getting a job is a critical step in building your version of the "American Dream". Whether you are from Denmark or Namibia, Sweden or Armenia, China or Hungary, Lebanon or India, Brazil, Russia, Mexico or any other country in the world, once you have arrived, you must understand and conform to the American way of job hunting in order to be successful.

When I arrived in America fifteen years ago, I had no idea how to look for a job . In my country (maybe in yours, too) you find work through the people you know, and those who owe favors to your family. I found that knowing the right people is also important in the US; however job hunting here works very differently — it is about **marketing yourself**. I learned this the hard way —by making mistakes and having to overcome and correct my misconceptions. That's why I decided to write this book: to help you avoid the mistakes I made and in the process save you months, maybe years of your valuable job search time.

As you read this book, you will see that looking for a job in the United States is a process. Once you know the process, it is easier to manage it, and you can be very successful in finding employment.

Although this book is directed primarily towards foreign nationals visiting the US, immigrants, and naturalized citizens (people with acquired American citizenship), anyone looking for a job (foreign or American born) will benefit from topics in the book such as crafting a resume, interview skills, and networking.

In addition to helping you with the basics of job hunting, the book offers tips on appropriate verbal and non-verbal behaviors that you can apply immediately —not only in your job search but in communicating in other areas of life in America. Again, the most important thing to remember throughout this process is that you are marketing *yourself*. I have written the book with one goal in mind – to help my readers develop the confidence, knowledge and tools to compete successfully in the American job market.

Job Hunting in America: Knowing the Rules

Do not be deceived by American informality —strict rules apply to the job search process. I designed this book to help you recognize and understand these rules, so that you can successfully market yourself and your professional skills. As I point out in the book, these rules can vary within business and academia, big corporations and small companies, and within different industries.

This book takes you through the basics of finding a job in the US. To succeed, i.e., to get those all-important job offers, you need the right tools. We will start with finding job openings and finish with how to negotiate a job offer.

How the book is organized

The book has eight chapters, followed by glossaries containing key words and phrases to help you understand general business and job search related terminology. A powerful vocabulary is one key to a successful job search. All chapters include a list of useful Websites and resources. Some chapters also have exercises to reinforce the knowledge and skills discussed. I recommend that you complete each exercise right after you read the chapter, to reinforce what you have just read.

Throughout the book you will find lists of useful resources and recommended literature for further study. Additional resources are listed on www.SucceedinAmerica.com website. A trip to your local library or bookstore will help you find more resources.

Icons used in this Book

Throughout "How to Get a Job in the USA," you will see several small symbols highlighting information that is useful, interesting or especially important to remember in your job search. So look for these icons throughout the book:

TIP FOR SUCCESS: *Specific information to help you succeed in your search.*

NOTE: *Behaviors or situations to be particularly aware of.*

STATISTICS: *Figures relating to the job market and related issues in the United States.*

COMPARISON: *Information comparing or contrasting the job market in the United States with that of other cultures.*

CAUTION! *Not in America! A reminder of a behavior or practice that is either considered unacceptable in America or is not part of the American culture.*

NOTE: These symbols are typical of those used in American culture. We understand that some images may be interpreted differently in other cultures, but these particular symbols were chosen because they are representative of the American way. In addition, the spelling, grammar and usage in this book reflect the American version of the English language.

After you read this book, I encourage you to supplement your learning by seeking more in-depth information by exploring the resources listed at the end of each section.

Postscript

Following her initial disappointments, Olga Petrovskaya received coaching from me on how to behave during the interview — what to wear, when and what questions to ask. In time, Olga got the job she deserved. She achieved her goal. Now it is your turn!

Chapter 1

THE HIRING PROCESS IN THE UNITED STATES

In this Chapter: ● The US job market ● Entering the US job market ● What do American employers look for? ● The qualities of an ideal American employee ● Communicating your abilities: resumes and interviews ● Six steps to getting hired in the US ● Who can work in the US? ● Fundamentals of getting established in the US: social security number, identification card, opening a bank account, establishing credit ● Speaking English in America ● American English ● How this book will help you ● Chapter glossary

The US Job Market

The United States is the wealthiest country in the world, with a dynamic, flexible, and mobile workforce. It is also the most popular destination in the world.

Despite the occasional crises, the US has a strong and vibrant economy. Specialists predict that in the coming years there will be an increasing demand for skilled workers to maintain that economy. Although job opportunities vary by field, and some American industries have moved their operations overseas, the current population will not be sufficient to meet this demand. This means that there will be plenty of job opportunities for immigrants and foreign nationals. You just need to know how to find them. From the following resources you can learn which professions are in demand and how to find jobs in your field:

- Networking with individuals employed in the same or similar industries
- Mass media — newspapers, television, radio and the Internet
- Employment agencies or "Headhunters" (agents who will match you with a professional position)
- Professional associations in your field and others (the Internet can be a useful tool for finding clubs and organizations in your area)
- US Government websites (such as BLS – Bureau of Labor Statistics, http://www.bls.gov/oco/)
- Jobs and careers websites.

A few words on current demand. Industries such as the hospitality industry (hotels and restaurants), healthcare (hospitals and doctor's offices) and information technology (programming, networks and computers) have the greatest need for foreign labor. Specialists predict that the shortage will increase in the years to come.

Does this mean that there are no opportunities for other professions? Not at all. For instance, although overall manufacturing is not a growing field, in the state of Connecticut right now there is already a shortage of skilled workers in manufacturing. In the state of Connecticut as of December 2005 there were 250,000 manufacturing jobs statewide, up over the previous year.

Entering the US Job Market

While searching for a job in the United States, always remember — job hunting in this country is all about marketing yourself. That's why this book emphasizes development of the types of verbal and non-verbal behavior that will help you to succeed.

The world has an abundance of well-trained professionals. You may have an advanced degree from a good school. You may have graduated at the top of your class. You may have superb academic credentials. These achievements, however, won't matter if you cannot effectively communicate your value to your target market — employers in the US.

NOTE
Job hunting in America is about marketing yourself effectively to employers.

What Do American Employers Look For?

To be successful in your job search, it is important to:

- Make sure you understand the hiring process from the employer's perspective.
- Know the qualities that American employers are looking for.
- Know how to convince them that you have those qualities.

First, it is important to differentiate between qualifications and personal qualities. *Qualifications, which are certified by diplomas and certificates, include your education, training and professional experience, job skills, and your past performance at work or school. Personal qualities include your character and personality, traits that are not ordinarily certifiable on a formal document.* Yet your character and personality, and how you behave or present yourself in various circumstances, are just as important as your qualifications when it comes to your image as a viable job candidate. You need to know how to present yourself in a positive way, and to highlight your ability to perform effectively.

Generally speaking, American employers look for employees who are competent, honest, reliable, flexible, energetic, self-starting, and self-confident. Other desirable qualities are effective communication, leadership, the ability to work well in a team, and enthusiasm. A global outlook, creativity and the ability to present your accomplishments (self-promotion) are also welcomed in a well-rounded candidate.

By now you are probably intimidated and think "How can I have all of these qualities?" Don't worry! I have described an ideal employee, but rarely does a candidate possess all of these qualities. Employers understand that candidates, like all people, have both strengths *and* weaknesses. The person selected for the job is the one who the employer perceives as having the greatest strengths and the fewest weaknesses.

COMPARE
Employers throughout the world share some of these values or requirements. However, different nations may have their own interpretations of them. The US has its own definition of qualities desirable in an employee.

To be successful in your job search you need to understand what behaviors American employers perceive as representing these desirable qualities. This book is about American ways and perceptions.

TIP FOR
SUCCESS!
In order to be successful in the US, you need to understand the American way of doing things. By emulating American ways you will project the specific qualities that are sought by US employers.

In the next section you will learn in more detail about the qualities of an ideal American employee. In subsequent chapters you will discover why these qualities are important, as well as some techniques for projecting these qualities.

The Qualities of an Ideal American Employee
(Qualities Required for the American Workplace)

Let's take a closer look at each of the qualities that describe an ideal employee. As I mentioned earlier, no one is expected to be ideal or perfect. Therefore try not to feel overwhelmed and compelled to become perfect. You might not possess all the qualities listed below; few people do. However, you do need to become familiar with the model American employee. This knowledge will help you to set and achieve your goals and to present yourself favorably during interviews. Above all, don't forget that the job search process in America is about self-marketing.

Self-Confidence

Projecting self-confidence is very important in the American workplace. In the US, people project confidence by keeping their posture straight, maintaining eye contact, keeping a relaxed, pleasant expression on their face, and smiling.

TIP FOR SUCCESS!

Keep in mind that a smile is a standard part of the greeting in the US. When you are greeting your interviewer, maintain eye contact, smile, and shake his/her hand.

Americans tend to think that everyone is this way, but many cultures are different. For example, Russians in formal situations typically do not smile. However, if you do not smile, Americans will interpret this as unhappiness, or think that you have a poor attitude. Who wants to hire someone who will appear unhappy or sullen on the job?

COMPARE

In some Latin American and Asian cultures, looking down when communicating with a prospective employer is a sign of respect. However, Americans may think that you lack confidence and/or have something to hide if you do not look a person in the eye.

Team Player

Many companies are organized into project teams to accomplish various tasks. This means that a team of people with different skill sets is required to accomplish a specific goal. You must be able to work with a variety of people in a team environment. Think of the word "team" as an acronym meaning Together Everyone Achieves More (TEAM). This concept originates from the American business culture.

Energy and Enthusiasm

Always project enthusiasm because this sends a positive message to the employer. American employers assume that an enthusiastic candidate will be a productive worker. And this is true most of the time. How can you project enthusiasm? Show that you are ready to learn, that you are not shy, and that you willingly accept a challenge. Make an effort to appear positive and excited about the prospective job. Americans define an energetic and enthusiastic worker as someone who will take the assignment, ask questions for clarification, and accomplish the task efficiently.

Leadership

Leadership is the ability to lead employees to accomplish business goals. Since American business is becoming more and more team and project oriented (especially in service industries), leadership skills are increasingly valuable. Those who possess good leadership skills are more likely to be promoted in the American workplace. An effective leader in the US motivates and encourages employees and helps them to grow professionally, using a positive attitude, lending support, and leading by example.

The Ability to Communicate Effectively

Good verbal communication skills are of great importance in the United States. In the workplace Americans will not take you seriously if you are unable to articulate your thoughts or opinions. You may be the best accountant or engineer, but if you cannot express this fact, the recruiter will not realize it. Naturally, your ability to express yourself clearly and insightfully has a great impact on the result of the interview.

**TIP FOR
SUCCESS!**

The organization Toastmasters International can help you build or improve your leadership and communication skills. These are the two top skills in the American workplace. Find a club in your area or country by going to www.toastmasters.org or calling the headquarters at (949) 958-8255.

Creativity

Creativity is the ability to be imaginative and to look at a situation from a new perspective. In the American workplace, you will often hear the expression "thinking outside the box," which means to think creatively. It means possessing the ability to look beyond the usual way of doing things (that's what "the box" means in this context). It means suggesting a new idea or taking a risk to develop an innovative solution to a workplace problem.

Adaptability and Flexibility

As the rate of change accelerates in all workplaces, the ability to adapt to new situations and tasks becomes critically important. Companies want to hire people who can embrace change, maintain a positive attitude throughout a transitional period, and implement new processes and procedures quickly.

Global Outlook/Understanding Diversity

Knowing one or more foreign languages and being able to work with people from other cultures is becoming ever more important as businesses expand throughout the world and employees move from country to country. More than ever before, the American workplace is a multi-cultural environment —this can work to your advantage!

Being Positive and Optimistic

A positive, optimistic outlook is a key value in American culture. Even a failure can be viewed as a stepping-stone to success, if one has learned from the experience. Never talk negatively about your country of origin, past job, manager or co-worker at the interview.

CAUTION!

Never speak negatively about your country of origin, past job, manager or co-worker. American employers view negative speech as a shortcoming.

Self-Promotion

Last, but far from least, you must be able to articulate your successes and accomplishments. In your culture this might seem like boasting, but if you do not mention your successes and accomplishments (big or small), an American employer may think that you do not have any. For more on how to present your accomplishments effectively, see Chapter 5, PROMOTING YOURSELF CONFIDENTLY AT THE INTERVIEW (Step 4), *Talking about Your Accomplishments*.

In addition to the qualities listed above, being *proactive* (or action-oriented), having *the ability to prioritize*, and being *innovative* contribute to the definition of an ideal American employee.

Communicating your abilities: resumes and interviews

We have just discussed the main qualities American employers look for in their employees. Now let's look at two critical steps in the job-hunting process, the resume and the job interview. These steps are critical because they are your opportunities to communicate your qualifications and qualities.

What is a resume? In America, a resume is a one- or two-page summary of your education, work experience, and other qualifications for a particular job. It helps employers determine whether they should consider you as a job candidate. A good resume is the first thing that you need to find employment in this country. The goal of the resume is to get you an interview. Therefore, the resume should attract the employer's attention by listing the qualifications that the employer is looking for. In Chapter 2 we will explain how to do that.

COMPARE

In some countries (for example, some Eastern European countries), an equivalent to the formal resume either does not exist, or is a new concept. In other countries, a resume is an extensive document with many pages of information about the job seeker.

What is an interview? An interview is a meeting between a job applicant and a potential employer. The purpose of an interview is to further assess the applicant's qualifications and suitability for the job. In other words, an interview is a conversation, a dialogue during which the job applicant convinces the employer that he or she can fulfill the job requirements, solve problems for the employer, and be a good fit for the company.

Resumes and interviews will be discussed in detail in Chapters 2, 4 and 5.

Six steps to getting hired in the United States

Now that we have introduced two fundamental elements of a job search — a resume and an interview — let's talk about what it takes to find suitable employment in the US. Learn the following six steps, and you are on your way.

Keep in mind that you can work on some of these steps simultaneously and they may not need to happen in the order listed below. For instance, you can work on your resume while you are working on your interviewing skills.

Step 1	Assemble your documentation	Identification/work permit application resume credentials (diplomas, certifications) cover letter (modified for each job)	See Chapter 2

Step 2	Find job openings	newspaper - classified section employment services/headhunters Internet networking	See Chapter 3
Step 3	Prepare for the interview	research the company know what to bring know how to dress compile Q&A practice Q &A	See Chapter 4
Step 4	Promote yourself confidently at the interview	introduction answer questions ask questions conclude	See Chapter 5
Step 5	Increase your chances by following up	write a thank you letter make follow up calls continue looking for jobs, submitting applications, etc.	See Chapter 6
Step 6	Finalize	the offer negotiate the job offer(s) accept /reject the offer (keep applying for jobs)	See Chapter 7

TIP FOR SUCCESS!

It's a numbers game: contact as many prospective employers as possible. Be patient! You will probably need to send many resumes before you are asked for an interview, and it may take several interviews before you are actually hired.

Who Can Work in the United States?

Before you start your job search, you need to know if you are legally allowed to work in the US, and how to obtain employment authorization. If you are a US citizen or a permanent resident (you have a document known as a "green card" which is actually of pink color), or you have refugee status, then you are automatically eligible for employment in the US.

If you are not a US citizen or do not have permanent residency, you will usually need to be in a non-immigrant category that allows you to work. Keep in mind that there are a variety of non-immigrant visa categories in the US. In the resources listed after this section, you will learn about the different types of non-immigrant visas that allow foreign nationals to work in the US. A person can either enter the US with the appropriate visa or, in some cases, change to the appropriate non-immigrant category once here.

Chapter 1

Employment authorization is a permission to work for monetary compensation in a country-specific currency. Certain types of visas imply permission to work under certain conditions or for a certain company.

NOTE!

Certain countries' nationals can enter the US without a visa; they can qualify for visa waivers. If you are from one of these countries, you do not need a visa for business and pleasure stays up to 90 days in duration. Most European countries, some Latin American countries, and Japan qualify for visa waivers. Most tourist visas prohibit working for compensation. Business travelers can do consulting or training but cannot do work that would typically be compensable.

A visa (as a rule stamped in a passport) will let you cross the border into the country, but being able to work legally in the US is a different matter. If you are planning to work in the US, you will need to apply for a non-immigrant visa that allows employment. Only holders of these work visas are legally allowed to work in the US. Keep in mind that work visas will have certain restrictions. Holders of other categories of visas are generally not permitted to accept any type of employment.

Most work visas allow employment for only one specific company. If your profession and qualifications are in demand in the US, a potential employer may agree to sponsor work for a work visa (for instance, H1-B or L-1 visa) for a defined period of time. Be aware that not all positions qualify for work visas and work visas have certain restrictions. Holders of other categories of visas are generally not permitted to accept any type of employment.

Another way to work legally is to obtain special permission with an EAD (Employment Authorization Document). Examples of who may qualify for EAD cards are non-citizen spouses and children (under 21 years of age) of US citizens who are applying for green cards. Students holding F-1 visas also may qualify for employment authorization for a limited time as well.

In the US, the working visa and work permit are combined into one document. If you are in the appropriate visa category, you do not need a separate "work permit." The US is unique in this aspect; most countries keep the visa and the work permit separate from each other. There are several visa categories in this country that allow for employment. For example, a B visa holder cannot work; an L-1 visa holder can.

COMPARE

Also note that if you have family living in the US, you are eligible to apply for permanent residency. However, there are certain limitations here, and it is a good idea to get a professional advice.

Since every situation is different, you might wish to consult an immigration attorney to understand your options. At the end of this section you will find a list of resources for finding immigration firms specializing in bringing in foreign nationals into the United States.

You can obtain (for a fee) competent immigration assistance through the countrywide members of the American Immigration Attorney Association (AILA), website www.aila.org. There are also organizations in many cities and states, such as the International Institute of Connecticut in Bridgeport, CT, International Institute of Buffalo, New York and other agencies recognized by the US Board of Immigration Appeals that provide free or low-cost immigration services for certain types of cases. You can go on IRSA's website (IRSA stands for Immigration and Refugee Services of America) www.irsa-uscr.org or www.refugee.usa.org, to find out if a partner organization exists in the state in which you live.

A list of recognized agencies is available at all local BCIS (Bureau of Citizenship and Immigration Service) offices. Below, you will find a listing of books and Websites that can help you locate these services and guide you through the immigration process.

Resources and literature:

Baldwin, Carl. *Immigration Questions and Answers.* Allworth Press, 3rd edition, 2002
Kimmel, Barbara Brooks, Allan M. Lubiner. *Immigration Made Simple: An Easy-to-Read Guide to the US Immigration Process.* Next Decade Inc., 2002
Liebman, Henry. *Getting into America.* How To Books: Plymouth, UK, 1999

Useful websites:

www.usdoj.gov/eoir/probono/states.htm – US Department of Justice Website provides a listing of free or low-cost immigration legal assistance.
www.aila.org – American Immigration Lawyers Association
http://www.ailf.org/imms/im_legal.asp – American Immigration Law Foundation
www.bcis.gov – Bureau of Citizenship and Immigration Services (BCIS). Among other helpful facts, the site provides information on the policies, procedures, forms, and fees involved in immigrating to the US. It also lists non-profit agencies providing services to immigrants and refugees.
http://www.refugeesusa.org - Immigration and Refugee Services of America (IRSA), assists refugees and immigrants in relocating to the United States.

Fundamentals of Getting Established in the US: Social Security Number, Identification Card, Opening a Bank Account, Establishing Credit

Once you have obtained a visa (H1-B, L-1 or any other type enabling you to work in the US), you are ready to take the following steps toward establishing yourself in the United States:

1. Acquire a Social Security card.
2. Obtain a driver's license or identification card.
3. Open a bank account.
4. Open a credit card account/Establish credit.
5. Buy or lease a car (if you do not live near access to public transportation).
6. Locate and finance a place to live (rent or buy a home).

The most pressing concerns are the first two steps: acquiring a Social Security number and driver's license or identification card (in that order). You can accomplish the remaining four steps in the order and timeframe that suits your needs.

Social Security Number. Your Social Security card, containing your nine-digit personal identification number, will be your key to many services and benefits in the US. In most cases, you will need your Social Security number to apply for school, work, a bank account, as well as to get a driver's license or a loan to buy a car or a home.

Social Security is a federal system guaranteeing at least some pension for people aged 65 or over. In the US, each wage earner automatically contributes a portion of his or her wages or salary to the Social Security Administration. The administration keeps track of how much you contribute throughout your lifetime, and when you turn 65, you become eligible to receive your pension. Participation in this system is mandatory, and therefore you cannot be legally employed in this country without a valid Social Security number.

NOTE!

You can apply for social security number only after you have received your visa and crossed the US border. To apply for the Social Security number, visit the nearest Social Security office. There are more than 1300 social security offices across the country so you do not have to travel far to find one. You can locate an office nearest you, as well as download necessary forms, by visiting the Social Security Administration Website at www.ssa.gov.

Driver's License or Identification Card. A driver's license, which doubles as an identification (ID) card, is the next most important personal card after your Social Security number. Normally you will need to apply for a driver's license within 30 days of arriving in the US. However, each state has specific requirements; and you should check the rules with the Department of Motor Vehicles in your state. Visit the official website for Motor Vehicle Administration (MVA) or Department of Motor Vehicles (DMV) or Department of Taxation or similar http://www.onlinedmv.com for downloadable forms and information. You can also call the 800-number (look it up in the local phone book or call information at 1-800-555-1212 to get the number) to find out the rules that apply in your state. If you do not drive, you can get a non-driver's identification card. In this case you will not need to take the drivers tests.

Bank Account. A bank account is another necessity when getting established in the US. You need a checking account to be able to write checks for goods and services. Try to open a bank account as soon as possible after your arrival in the US. You will need a valid identification document (ID), a mailing address and some funds with which to make an initial deposit. Generally speaking, you need a Social Security number to open a bank account in the US. However, some banks will open an account without one. They will ask you to complete an IRS form W-8 instead. Setting up a savings account in a savings bank or credit union in the US is the fastest way to start building credit. Read on.

Establishing Credit. Once you have a social security number, you are able to apply for all other necessities. A fundamental requirement is to establish a credit history in the US. If you do not have a credit history in this country or enough money in the bank, you will not be able to finance a car or any other major item (such as buying a home).

NOTE! *Credit is a form of deferred payment. Normally you will be charged interest for the privilege of buying something on credit unless you pay within a predetermined timeframe.*

Generally, it is hard to get credit immediately upon coming to the US, even if you have a good credit history in your country. Sometimes it can take a number of years. A good resource to get credit building advice is the National Foundation for Credit Counseling (NFCC). The organization's website is www.nfcc.org. Another useful website is www.moneymanagement.org. NFCC member agencies are staffed with helpful consultants who will explain how best to go about establishing credit, what you will need to have, how to develop a budget, etc. In the US you can reach NFCC at 1-800-388-2227 and find a credit counseling agency in your area. Some agencies are able to give credit building advice nationally. One of those agencies is Money Management International – in the US call 1-866-889-9348.

As a rule, American credit bureaus will not be able to check the credit that you established in your home country. In rare cases, however, if an employer provides a proof of employment, or you can provide some documentation from your home country, you may be able to open a limited credit line soon after you arrive in the US. If you come from a part of the world where credit use is uncommon, it can be even more difficult to establish credit in the US. This could change, however, as credit companies are realizing that many foreigners entering the US are looking for faster ways to build a credit history.

Once in the United States, it can be very hard to finance your car. A way to do it is to start building a US credit history before you arrive. One company that helps you do this is *International AutoSource*. Purchasing a car from *International AutoSource* is one way of establishing credit. This company offers a choice of several American-made car brands at wholesale prices, and can help those without a credit history to obtain financing and auto insurance. Remember that you will be accomplishing two things: obtaining a vehicle *and* establishing a credit history for later use. Keep in mind is that you must make the initial contact with this company *prior* to your arrival in the US. To learn more about the company and what it offers, visit www.intlauto.com. Read further how you can establish credit while in the US.

Here are a few ways to build your credit from scratch in the US.

- Your utility bill could be a starting point to build credit. Pay your bills on time. Phone, gas and electricity companies report unpaid or late bills to credit bureaus such as Experian, Equifax and TransUnion.
- A very good way to build credit is to obtain a credit card using a savings deposit as collateral.
- Explore options to get a secured credit card with a bank or credit union where you have your own savings. In this case your savings will be used to guarantee your payment.

Useful Websites and Resources

www.nfcc.org – 1-800-388-2227, a good resource to get credit building advice is the National Foundation for Credit Counseling (NFCC).

www.creditcounseling.org – Consumer Credit Counseling of Southern New England – in the US call 1-800-208-2227.

www.moneymanagement.org – 1-866-889-9348, Consumer Credit Counseling Service; also offers educational services.

Obtaining a Credit Card. A credit card allows you to purchase products and services without having to pay your money at the time of purchase. This is called buying *on credit*. The credit card company pays the bill for you. In time, you repay the credit card company in monthly installments or, if you prefer, pay off the entire balance owed. If you choose to pay the bill in installments, the credit card company will charge you monthly interest payments (a predetermined percentage of the purchase price). When you are trying to establish credit, it is very important to pay your monthly credit card bill on time. Therefore, each month always pay at least the "minimum amount due' on your credit card statement by the "payment due date". Do not miss a payment because that will jeopardize your credit rating. Keep in mind, if you do not pay in full, you will be charged interest.

It is not easy to function without credit cards in the US as well as in many other parts of the world. Even if you have cash, a credit card is still required to purchase a plane ticket or a hotel room. Getting a credit card is an important step to building credit. The credit card brands most commonly accepted in the US are Visa, MasterCard and American Express.

Chapter 1

Speaking English in America

> *"If you want to reach your goals, you need to change your vocabulary."*
> — *Zig Ziglar, motivational speaker and author*

I would add to Mr. Ziglar's statement "… and grammar, and accent, and speaking skills." Good English language skills will greatly improve your chances of employment in the United States. English proficiency is particularly important if you are looking for a job that requires you to be on the telephone frequently, or requires verbal interaction or presentation skills. For instance, you will be expected to speak fluent English for customer service jobs.

A good measure of your language skill is your ability to engage in basic discussions about the industry or field you are attempting to enter and "small talk" (casual non-business related conversation). If a potential employer contacts you by telephone, you should be able to converse in English.

You must also demonstrate a willingness to improve your language skills. There are different ways of doing this. You can enroll in English language classes, join a speaking club (such as **Toastmasters**); or take a commercial course (see the list of commercial courses below). Commercial courses are more expensive, but are more likely to emphasize business English skills. Some non-profit organizations, such as Literacy Volunteers of America, provide quality business English courses for a more moderate fee.

Many public libraries and adult education units in the US have thriving ESL (English as a Second Language) programs. Some libraries may offer computer-assisted, interactive language teaching programs such as ELLIS or English Discoveries series. Continuing education in many colleges and universities throughout the US offer ESL and business communication classes.

There are exceptions—not all jobs require English proficiency. In addition, your ability to speak a foreign language could be a great asset if your potential employer has non-English speaking customers.

Further Resources:

Adult Education – go on-line and type in "adult education" and your city and state in your favorite search engine to locate adult education opportunities in your area.

Berlitz – www.berlitz.com. Berlitz provides language instruction throughout numerous locations in the US.

Cendant Intercultural – www.cendantmobility.com (select the link to: Cendant Intercultural). To contact by phone, call: 1-800-251-9005, (312) 251-9000. This company provides business and general English communication courses for corporate employees and their families. Programs are generally tailored to specific individual needs and delivered practically in any US location. Although Cendant Intercultural does not deal with individuals directly, if you are being relocated to the US by your employer, you can request language training to be arranged and delivered by Cendant.

Inlingua – www.inlingua.com. Inlingua centers offer comprehensive language training in many US locations.

Literacy Volunteers of America, Inc. (LVA) – LVA is a national network of local, state, and regional literacy providers. LVA's cost-effective system enables them to provide student-focused language tutoring, one-to-one or in small groups. To find an LVA branch in your area, visit **www.literacyvolunteers.org** or call headquarters at (202) 792-8260.

American English

You may have studied English in high school or college. Although you may be able to speak, write and understand English competently, the English that you know may not be exactly the same language that Americans speak. And it may not be sufficient in the workplace. The ability to read Charles Dickens' novels in their original form may be impressive to some, but employers are looking for people who can communicate clearly and effectively with their co-workers and customers, read technical manuals, and write office memos and e-mails in 21st century standard American English.

American and British English speakers understand each other most of the time. However, if you use British words or expressions that are not used in the same way in the US, you are likely to get blank or confused looks from your American colleague. The differences range from sentence structure to word meanings and use of expressions.

If you have learned British English or other versions of the English language, you need to know how American English differs. Otherwise, there will be misunderstandings, miscommunication, and possibly even embarrassment.

A handy reference for acquiring good idiomatic vocabulary is Barron's *Handbook of American idioms*. Another resource is *Ameri$peak,* which contains a concise and comprehensive list of idioms and acronyms widely used in American Business English. It is a short dictionary that contains the most common words and phrases you need to know to communicate effectively in American business. (See the specifics in the resources at the end of this Chapter and the order form at the end of this book).

TIP FOR SUCCESS!

To communicate effectively in the US, a newcomer needs to speak and understand the American version of the English language.

Today's American job market requires non-natives to speak and understand the American version of the English language. In the future however, the many Americans will work with foreign-born people. Consequently, it is becoming more important in the US to understand foreign cultures. The statistics and facts shown below illustrate this point.

STATISTIC

More than 10% of Americans were born outside the US. English is not the primary language for 15% of Americans.
30 million people speak a second language at home (18 million are Spanish speakers).
Many ethnic communities have their own newspapers, radio and TV stations and worship religion in their own language.

Note: Because statistics become outdated, visit the US Census Bureau website (www.Census.gov) for the most current information on US demographics.

Useful resources and literature:

Ameri$peak (The Most Common Words And Phrases You Need To Know To Communicate Effectively In American Business). Succeed In America, 2006. See the order form at the end of this book. Also can be ordered through **www.SucceedinAmerica.com**.
Borunda, Dileri. *Speak American.* A survival guide to language and culture in the USA. Johnston. Random House: New York, 2000
Handbook of Commonly used American Idioms. Barron's, New York, 1995.
Hampshire, David. *Living and Working in America.* Survival Books, London, England, 2002.

Chapter 1

Mikatavage, Raimonda. *Immigrants and Refugees.* Create your new life in America. USA, 1998

Nolan, Riall W. *Communicating and Adapting across Cultures.* Living and Working in the Global Village. Bergin & Gaervey. Westport, Connecticut, London.

Priven, Judy. *Hello!USA. Everyday Living for International Residents and Visitors.* Hello! America, Inc. 1999

www.toastmasters.org – an international organization with more than 8,000 clubs worldwide dedicated to improving and building communication and leadership skills

How This Book Will Help You

To summarize Chapter 1, we have learned that there are many job opportunities in the US, yet even more people applying for them. Despite impressive credentials, many qualified jobseekers do not find suitable employment for a long time. Although luck plays a role in this, most of these people remain unemployed because they do not understand the job search process, can't speak everyday American English, and lack the skills and knowledge to present themselves favorably to prospective employers.

By the time you finish reading this book, you will have acquired the skills necessary to successfully compete for the job of your choice. You will learn to avoid the mistakes that prevent others from achieving their goals. You will also discover how easy it is to acquire those skills. Now, let's get started with your job search!

Chapter Glossary

Accomplishments: professional tasks successfully completed

Adapt to: adjust to changing environment

Applicant: job candidate; person applying for a job

Application: a set of documents, including a resume, and the application form used as a document to apply for a job opening

Articulate (verb): to pronounce distinctly and carefully

Articulate (adj): endowed with the power of speech; well-spoken

Association (professional association): organization of people with same interest or profession

Attorney: a lawyer

BCIS: Bureau of Citizenship and Immigration Service

Behavior: way of acting

Blank look (to get a blank look): facial expression signaling misunderstanding

Candidate: a job applicant, an interviewee

Certificate: a document confirming ability to perform certain work

Classified ad (newspaper classified): newspaper advertisement for employment opportunities

Competent: professionally able

Cover letter: a letter of introduction accompanying a job application and resume

Credentials: qualifications (including diplomas, etc.)

Credit: amount of money you can get in advance

Culture: values; beliefs; traditions; customs; a way of doing things

Diploma: a document issued by an educational institution testifying that a student earned a degree

Domestically: within the United States

Dynamic: forceful and changing, variational and energetic

E-mail: electronic message via Internet

Employer (recruiter, interviewer): a person making or participating in the hiring decision

Employment: working in return for financial compensation

Embrace change: to accept change

Enthusiasm: eagerness; zeal; positive energy

Fill a position: to hire someone for an open position

Flexible: adaptable to change

Fluent (English): can discuss any topic in virtually any situation

Globally: throughout the world, internationally and nationally

Headhunter: an executive recruiter

ID: identification document

Interview: a meeting or a conversation between a job applicant and a potential employer to assess the applicant's suitability for the job

Job-hunting: job search

Job offer: an official offer to accept the job

Job opening: a job or position that is not filled

Job opportunities: job openings

Job seeker: a person looking for a job

Leadership: an ability to lead people (generally in a team and/or project)

Leadership skills: ability to motivate and organize people for successful work

License (occupational license): a certificate from the government that a person is qualified to do a certain job

Manuals (technical manuals): instructions, reference book, business related descriptive document

Memo: an informational business communication

Networking: making connections with people to find information on job or other business-related opportunities

Newspaper classified: newspaper advertisement showing job or business opportunities

Opportunity: good chance, favorable circumstances (job opportunity = job opening)

Permanent Resident: a person holding a green card

Positive: optimistic

Proactive: initiating action

Proficient (in English): can hold extended conversations on an array of topics

Professional: projecting competence in a particular field; behaving in a mature, polished manner

Project (noun): a task requiring joint effort

Project (verb) **confidence:** appear confident or self-assured

Q&A: questions and answers

Qualifications: proof of ability to perform certain jobs, skills

Refugee: a person in exile

Regroup: reorganize, restructure, get reorganized, get restructured

Resume: a document summarizing education, experience and qualifications

Self-promotion: ability to present oneself favorably

Self-starter: go-getter, doer, hard worker

Skilled labor: work demanding advanced training

Skills: talents, abilities.

Team: A group of employees organized to work together

TEAM: Together Everyone Achieves More

Think outside the box: Be creative in business, be a problem solver

US citizen: US national

Verbal: Spoken; using language

Video-Conferencing Interview: An interview conducted with the help of videoconferencing technology

Visa: travel document, stamp in the passport permitting travel to a given country

Work visa: travel document permitting employment

CHAPTER 2

STEP 1: ASSEMBLE YOUR RESUME AND DOCUMENTATION

In this Chapter: ● What you need to begin your job search ● The American resume basics ● Resume structure ●Action verbs ● Traditional resume formats ● Create your own resume ● Non-traditional resume types ● The cover letter ● Educational credentials and licensing ● The application form ● Moving On ● Chapter glossary

What You Need to Begin Your Job Search

Assuming that you are legally authorized to work in the US[1], there are a few basic documents you must have before you apply for almost any professional or office job in the US:

1. **A resume** customized towards each job for which you are applying

2. **Documentation of any professional training or credentials**, including on-the-job training and any formal training outside the US

3. **Cover letters** customized for each job application

4. Completed **application form** (not all employers will require this, but be prepared to fill one out)

Let's look at these four documents one-by-one.

The American Resume Basics

Your resume is the first important tool you will need in your job search. In America, your resume should be a one- or two-page summary of your education, work experience, and other qualifications for a particular job. It is your ad. It is also your "passport" to get your foot in the door of the employer. Just as a proper passport is required to cross international borders, a strong, convincing resume is essential for getting you the opportunity to interview for the job. If you are looking for a professional or office job, a resume is the first item employers and recruiters need from you when you come to them in your job search. Unless you can rely on your network or a recruitment agency to get you an interview, you will be selected or rejected for the interview based on the content of your resume alone. Therefore a presentable resume is the first key step to your successful job search. Like a passport, you simply won't get very far without it.

NOTE! *A resume in academia is called curriculum vitae or CV. In this case, the resume will typically be longer than one or two pages and will contain a list of publications, presentations at conventions, and other accomplishments.*

COMPARE *A resume is a summary, including only highlights, and it is not detail oriented. A CV is the opposite. It is a complete accounting of one's professional life in all its detail. A CV may run 10-30 pages, especially for someone having many publications.*

---

[1] See Chapter 1, *Who Can Work in the US?*

Resume Structure

Creating a resume that will get you to Step 2 - an interview – is critical. Let's get started. Remember that you will be chosen or rejected for an interview based on information in your resume.

NOTE!

As a minimum, your resume should contain your contact information, past job and volunteer experiences related to your occupation, and education.

A typical resume in the US includes the following components: contact information, employment objective (optional), work experience, education, accomplishments, special skills, publications and references. Let's look at each of these elements in detail.

Contact Information

List your name, address, phone number, e-mail.

TIP FOR SUCCESS!

Make sure that you have an answering machine or voice mail. Record a clear and a professional greeting. A missed phone call is an opportunity lost! (See Chapter 8, Phone Skills. Creating a Professional Greeting).

COMPARISON

Personal information such as age, marital status or religion is not appropriate on an American resume. Moreover, because of current discrimination laws in the US, they can lead to a lawsuit against the employer.

In some countries it is common practice to include your date of birth, marital status, and even a photo of yourself. In one European country, 10 percent of all hiring decisions are made based on numerology!

Employment Objective (Optional)

Including a statement of objective can help give the prospective employer a better sense of your professional goals. Keep this statement fairly broad and non-specific; you don't want your goals to seem too limited. Here is an example.

> *Objective: To obtain a position in a company where my experience, skills and accomplishments will allow me opportunities for growth in the areas of Training and Development, Program Development, or Language Interpreting.*

Work Experience/Past Employment

List each job. Put down how long you held each position. Include the city and country if it was outside the US, and for US-based jobs, list the city and state. Include relevant details of your duties, responsibilities, and accomplishments on the job as they relate to the position for which you are applying. (See the resume samples in this chapter).

If you have done any volunteer work that is relevant to the desired position, make sure to mention it. For instance, if you are applying for a language teaching position, and you taught English as a volunteer, include this information!

If you have any time gaps in your employment history (e.g., you had a baby or you have recently relocated to America and did not work for some time), be prepared to explain why you did not work and what you were doing during that time.

Education

List any degree or special courses that show you are qualified in your field. Indicate where you received your education. If you were educated in another country, you may need to have your degrees evaluated for a US equivalent. (e.g., a Ph.D. acquired in the countries of the former Soviet Union might be equated to a Master's Degree, unless the individual is recognized in his or her field and has published widely).

Later in this chapter, we will focus more closely on how educational credentials are evaluated in the US. When describing your education, be brief and concise, but also be prepared to clearly explain your education in terms that American employers will understand.

(Selected) Accomplishments

This section demonstrates what you have achieved during your professional life. Write a list of your accomplishments in your past work or educational career (e.g., *"Developed a training program for new hires"*). To emphasize your achievements, you should quantify them whenever possible (e.g., *"Improved production process that decreased manufacturing costs by 25 percent."*). Accomplishments may be listed as a separate section or within each job or skill set.

Your Special Skills

Highlight your special abilities, especially computer and language skills if you have them. List any other skills or experiences relevant to the job. For example, if you are applying for a position that involves international travel, describe your experiences living and working in a multi-cultural environment.

When listing your language skills, always mention the degree of fluency for each language; e.g., English – *fluent*, Italian – *conversational*. Below are some general guidelines for clearly defining your language abilities.

NOTE!

Definitions of language proficiency levels:
Fluent – can discuss any topic
Proficient – can hold extended conversations on an array of topics
Conversational – can hold short conversations on simple topics in limited contexts
Basic – can use a few words, some simple memorized phrases

Publications and Article Titles

If you have been published in professional journals or magazines, or written books relevant to the position you seek, be sure to include a bibliography along with the professional experience listed in your resume.

Related Memberships

If you belong to any professional organizations, list them (e.g., The International Society of Language Teachers or Mechanical Engineers Association of Spain.).

References

References are people who can testify as to what kind of worker you are or simply confirm your professional history. The recruiter or prospective employer may contact your references to verify the information that you have already stated in your resume and/or interview. They may also ask your reference for his or her professional opinion of you.

It is not customary to include references along with your resume. However, always keep ready a list of references on a separate sheet of paper. Below is an example of a basic references sheet.

REFERENCES FOR VIVIANA FARIAS

Robert H. Baldrich
President
Executive Jetport
(203) 855-1XXX
(608) 883-2XXX

Sofia Mires
Account Manager for the Americas
General Electronics, Inc.
(201) XXX-163X

Janis C. Nicholas
Executive Director
Connecticut Global Trade Association
(203) XXX-55X5

Lauren M. Ponce
President
Language Express
(203) XXX-323X

Resume Do's

Here are some additional tips for preparing a good resume:

1. Check your resume for spelling mistakes and grammar. It is extremely important to make a great first impression. The perception is that a person who did not take time to spell-check the resume will not be a conscientious employee.

2. If you send your resume by mail, your cover letter and envelope should be of the same color and quality as your resume. Use a good quality white or off-white 8.5 × 11 inch (22 cm × 28.5 cm) paper.

3. Use professional layout and formatting.

4. Use bullets whenever appropriate.

5. How long should your resume be? Many companies prefer a one- or two-page resume. However, if you had many jobs or are seeking a position in academia, and have a number of publications, your resume can be longer.

6. Use action verbs to describe your experiences and accomplishments. (See below for more information on action verbs.

Chapter 2

Action Verbs

By using action verbs to state your accomplishments, your resume becomes more powerful because you are creating a dynamic picture of your achievements. A short list of action verbs appears below. Note that, with the exception of your current job, the verbs in your resume should be used in the past tense. It does make sense, right? Use action verbs as often as possible.

TIP FOR SUCCESS! *In the American action-oriented culture, using action verbs helps convey a positive impression.*

A Short List of Common Action Verbs

- Accelerated, achieved, adapted, analyzed, arranged
- Budgeted, built
- Created, calculated, coached, compiled, completed, computed, conceptualized, consulted, coordinated
- Delivered, designed, determined, developed, devised, directed, distributed
- Established, evaluated, examined, executed, expanded, expedited
- Facilitated, founded
- Generated
- Headed
- Identified, implemented, improved, increased, influenced, initiated, installed, instituted, instructed, integrated, invented
- Launched, led, leveraged, served as a liaison
- Maintained, managed, manufactured, marketed, mediated, mentored, monitored, motivated
- Negotiated
- Obtained, operated, orchestrated, ordered, organized
- Participated, performed, planned, prepared, presented, processed, produced, proposed, provided
- Reduced, represented, researched, restructured, revised
- Saved, scheduled, served, serviced, strategized, streamlined, supervised, supplied
- Targeted, tested, trained
- Updated, unified
- Validated
- Wrote

Traditional Resume Formats[2]

Two of the most common (traditional) ways to organize resumes are: chronological and functional. Let's take a look at each of the two formats.

---

[2] By traditional resumes we mean the types that are typically mailed or faxed to prospective employers along with a cover letter. Later in this chapter, we will discuss other "non-traditional" types of resumes.

Chronological Resume

This is the most common resume style. In this style, you list your experience in reverse chronological order (i.e., starting with the most recent). Keep in mind that different types of resumes can produce different results depending on your situation.

NOTE!   *If you have just graduated from a college and have limited or no employment experience (or no recent experience), list your education first, starting with the most recent.*

The advantage of this style is that it is clear and easy to read. It is especially recommended if you have held two or more jobs in the same field, or you have been building your skills steadily in a certain area and the job you are applying for relates directly to those skills. A few samples of chronological resumes follow.[3]

Functional Resume

A functional resume lists your skills in groups. In other words, it places emphasis on what you can *do*, and on *your developed and transferable skills, and experiences* rather than the time, place and order in which you obtained them.

The functional resume may be for you if you are:

- Entering the US job market after a gap in your employment history, due (for instance) to relocation or a need to build your language skills; or
- Changing careers

An examples of functional resumes follows.

---

[3] Some of the sample resumes in this book were designed with the help of Alfred J. Mariani, M.B.A., Résumés Etc., of Trumbull, Connecticut.

Sample Chronological Resume

VIVIANA FARIAS

XX Old Town Road • Bridgeport, CT 06606 USA • Phone: (203) XXX-2229 • e-mail: af@aolx.com

SUMMARY: A translator/interpreter with 16 years of experience in corporate setting

WORK EXPERIENCE

- **Freelance Translator, Portuguese & Italian**
  Tele-Interpreter: OMNI Interpreting Services (Thousand Oaks, CA)   1997 – Present

- **Translator & Interpreter** for a Development Company
  UNITECH, S.A. (Greenwich, CT)   1994-1997

- **Teacher of Business and Technical Translation**
  BRAZILIAN POLYTECHNIC INSTITUTE (Sao Paulo, Brazil)   1981-1994

Selected Projects
- Translated numerous business, legal, and technical documents
- Interpreted and facilitated business negotiations
- Published 17 works on business and technical translation

Selected accomplishments

- **Interpreted business negotiations** between Brazilian Chamber of Commerce and All-American, Inc., New York, USA, 2004
- **Translated into Italian**. Who is Who & Business Proposals - International Academy for Leadership in Business and Administration, 1200 entries, 1995-1997
- **Translated into Portuguese**. Australia: Investment Opportunities, Business Program, 70 pages, Sydney, Australia, 1997
- **Translated into Portuguese.** USA: Construction Industry, 100 pages, New York, 1997

EDUCATION

Options Program - Accelerated computer and business courses - Gibbs College, Norwalk, CT, 1997

BA in Languages (Portuguese – English) – Universidade Paulista – UNIP, Sao Paulo, Brazil, 1991-1995

Italian language course – Advanced Level – Circolo Italiano de Sao Paulo, Sao Paulo, Brazil, 1991-1995

LANGUAGES: Portuguese/English/Italian/Spanish

MEMBERSHIPS AND VOLUNTEER WORK

- Student Liaison, American Translators Association
- Education VP, Toastmasters International, Diversity-USA Club, Danbury, CT

REFERENCES AVAILABLE UPON REQUEST

Sample chronological resume

ERICA Maria Fernandes
XX Hill Road, Middleberry, CT
Phone: 203-X91-XX77, E-mail: eXXf@aol.com

EDUCATION

2003-2006   **SCHOOL OF BUSINESS AT YORK UNIVERSITY**   York, New York
Master of Business Administration degree, June 2003
Field Study in International Business – Strategy Consulting Project in Asia, Dec 2002

1990-1995   **ESCOLA DE ADMINISTRACAO SAO PAULO**   Sao Paulo, Brazil
Top Business School in Brazil
B.A. in Business Administration, August 1991

EXPERIENCE

Summer 2005   **BANCO DE ESPANHA**   Sao Paulo, Brazil
Summer Associate, Investment Banking, Mergers & Acquisitions
- Conducted financial and valuation analysis (DCF, trading & transactions comps) and prepared an offer memorandum for a major Brazilian textile company
- Advised a large Spanish insurance company on its acquisition of a recently privatized insurance company in Brazil. Performed strategic and financial analysis of the business

2002-2005   **BANCO AMERICANO**   Sao Paulo, Brazil
Relationship Manager, Investor Services Division
- Managed foreign institutional investor account relationships valued at greater than US$1.5 billion
- Developed a sales strategy for selling back-office solutions to large domestic institutional investors
- Implemented the first domestic institutional investor portfolio valued at US$250 million

LANGUAGES
- Fluent in English and Portuguese (native); proficient in German and French

MEMBERSHIPS
- Member of Finance, Consulting, International and Women in Business Clubs
- Toastmasters International

Sample Functional Resume

German Vega

Rio Salinas 36 • Col Villa del Rio Monter N.L. Mexico • Phone: 52 8181 596
germanv@hotmail.com

QUALIFICATIONS

Business Development and Program Marketing

- Developed customer base via direct mail, telephone solicitations and personal contacts
- Generated interest among business leaders in sponsoring events with company clients
- Recruited companies, state, and federal organizations to participate in the events and cultivating new prospects
- Publicized business and educational events through media to attract potential participants

Operations and Project Management/Program Coordination

- Developed programs in Latin America, Europe and North America
- Coordinated with associates in Mexico and American organizations for planning and execution of business programs
- Arranged itineraries, invitations and visas
- Negotiated prices for services
- Balanced budgets to organizational guidelines

Selected Accomplishments

- Developed and executed 28 programs from development to management of on-site events
- Recruited organizations in the USA to sponsor company's clients, saving 25% on each program cost
- Saved $250,000 over three year period by negotiating supplier prices

Memberships

- Foreign Trade Association
- Mexican Chamber of Commerce

EMPLOYMENT HISTORY

ITI, Inc. – Account Manager, a training company, Bridgeport, CT, 2000 – present
Unitech s.a. – Interpreter, an international trading company, Greenwich, CT, 1998 – 2000
Meslie Gold – Office Manager/Translator, Import Company, Greenwich, CT, 1996 – 1997

EDUCATION

Sacred Heart University, CT, USA, MBA Program, 1999
University of Mexico, B.A., English language, 1989

REFERENCES AVAILABLE UPON REQUEST

Create Your Own Resume

Now, it's time to create your own resume! We'll begin with the chronological format. The next few pages contain a worksheet to guide you through the process. For help with filling out this worksheet, refer to *American Resume Basics,* found earlier in this chapter. Completing this worksheet will help you understand and make better use of information presented later in this book.

When you feel that you did your best, ask someone who has experience with American resumes to critique and proofread your resume. Keep editing until it is polished and flawless. If this is your first attempt at creating yours, don't be discouraged if it takes you some time to become comfortable with it — as with any new skill, the more time you put into it, the more quickly you will be able to use it effectively. So don't give up if you aren't happy with your initial document. Just review the descriptions and examples, and try again. Good luck!

Resume Creation Worksheet
(Use additional sheets of paper for each section if necessary.)

1. HOW TO CONTACT YOU (your name, address, phone number, e-mail)

COMPARE

In the US, people list their first name first, then the family name, e.g., Diana Stephenson or Bob Brown. Also, unlike many other cultures, Americans are quite liberal about listing their nicknames in professional situations. You find that even CEO's or CFO's refer to themselves as Jerry instead of Gerald, Bob instead of Robert, or Pat instead of Patricia or Patrice.

TIP FOR SUCCESS!

If your name is very different from American names, consider incorporating American nicknames in parentheses, e.g., Hambartsum ("Eddie") Hovannisian, to make your name easier for others to remember and pronounce.

_____
_____
_____

2. YOUR OBJECTIVE (optional)

TIP FOR SUCCESS!

Put your objective into fairly general terms. Give employers a sense of your goals, but don't limit yourself by giving too many specifics.

_____
_____
_____

3. EXPERIENCE

Your past jobs (employer, location, position, responsibilities, dates). This may be an extensive section if you have held several jobs in the past. Add additional sheets of paper if needed. List the jobs in reverse chronological order (starting with the latest or current job)

Job 1.

POSITION_____

EMPLOYER_____

Job Location _____Dates (start and end)_____

RESPONSIBILITIES. (What did you do?). Use action verbs.

_____
_____
_____
_____

Job 2.

POSITION_____

EMPLOYER_____

Job Location _____Dates (start and end)_____

RESPONSIBILITIES. (What did you do?). Use action verbs.

_____
_____
_____
_____

Job 3, 4, etc.

4. EDUCATION

Emphasize the positive. If you are a college graduate with limited or no job experience, the education component should go before the experience section.

_____
_____
_____
_____

TIP FOR SUCCESS!

Whenever possible, use American English translations and brief descriptions of American equivalents for the name of the company or educational Institution; e.g., do not use "Candidate of Science", use instead "equivalent to US Master's Degree in Science".

5. Your accomplishments
List your accomplishments either separately or within each job experience.

_____
_____
_____
_____

6. Your special skills
List your special abilities that are relevant to your field of interest. This may include computer skills and/or language skills.

_____
_____
_____
_____

7. Names of publications and titles of articles or books to your credit (if applicable)

_____
_____
_____
_____

8. Names of professional organizations you belong to (if applicable)
List only memberships related to your prospective job. Sometimes, however, it is advisable to list volunteer experience as well, even if it is not directly related to the job. Many employers are interested in hiring people who care about the community. It contributes to a positive public image of the company.

_____
_____
_____
_____

9. References.
Simply type the phrase "**REFERENCES AVAILABLE UPON REQUEST**" at the bottom of your resume and type a list of your references on a separate sheet of paper (see the sample references sheet shown earlier in the chapter).

NOTE!

Bring your List of References to the interview and provide it only if the recruiter asks for references. Be sure your list of references has your name on it as the applicant so the recruiter knows who it belongs to in the event it gets misplaced from other information in your file.

Chapter 2

Congratulations! You have all of the information that you need to create your resume! Now, format your information, edit, and proofread it yourself. Be sure to ask someone familiar with American English to check it carefully once again. Then you can customize your cover letter, and you are on your way.

NOTE!

Very often you will be able to build a resume on the web; www.careerbuilder.com is one such website.

You can find a good selection of sample resumes in *Further Resources and Literature* in the next section. A trip to your local library or local bookstore will help you find more resources. Chose a resume close to your field of interest and use it (in combination with the above worksheet) as a starting point to compose and improve your own. Be prepared to talk to your prospective employers about everything you present in your resume.

If you choose not to write the resume yourself, there are plenty of professional resume writers available to write it for a fee. Some are better than others, so always ask to see samples. If possible, get a recommendation from someone you know. If you are in the US, you can find resume writers in your local business phone book and on the Internet. There are also Websites that will help you learn even more about effective resume writing. Whether you decide to write your own resume or seek professional help, some sites that can get you started are listed below.

www.nrwa.com – the National Resume Writers' Association (NRWA) Website. The site lists resume consultants in the US and some countries.

http://provenresumes.com – tips for different resume types

www.parw.com – Professional Association of resume writers and career coaches. On this website you can find a certified resume writer.

www.resume.com – Career services provider specializing in resumes. If you are in the US, you can call toll-free 1-800-resumes (1-800-737-8637)

Non-traditional Resume Types

The resume types described in the previous section are often called *traditional* resumes because they are printed on paper by the job applicant and mailed or faxed to employers. While traditional resumes are still widely used, more and more employers today are asking for resumes that can be processed with the help of technology. These *non-traditional* resumes types include scannable, electronic, e-mail and Web-resumes. Understanding how resume scanning and tracking systems work will dramatically increase your chance of success.

Scannable Resumes

A scannable resume is simply one that can be scanned into a computer. Many large employers scan resumes into a database to keep them on file for future use. Scannable resumes allow companies to search quickly through a large number of applicants by searching for *key words*. A key word is a term or a buzzword commonly used within an industry — and they are one of the most important aspects of the scannable resume. Employers type in a key word, and all of the resumes containing that word will appear on the screen. Now you can see what an advantage it is to have those magic words on your resume! It's a numbers game: the more relevant key words in your resume, the higher it will be ranked. The higher your ranking, the greater the chance your resume will be chosen for further consideration.

Through research and networking, you may be able to find out which key words the company requires. If you use them in the resume appropriately and frequently enough, they will trigger the recruiter's attention and increase the chances that your resume will be read.

The following examples illustrate key words for each of two different positions.

- Chemical Engineer Position: chemistry, hazardous material, microbiology, chemical process, process engineering, fuel cells, environmental, etc.
- Administrative Assistant Position: Microsoft Office, Excel, Coordination, PowerPoint, word-processing, appointment, scheduling, etc.

A scannable resume format needs to be simple so that a computer recognizes the words and does not distort the meaning. Here are some recommendations for writing your scannable resume:

Do:	Do not:
Use nouns instead of action verbs	Do not use graphics
Use black ink on white paper	Do not use two-column layout
Mail it in a large envelope (because it cannot be folded or stapled)	Do not fold or staple it
	Do not use bold, italics, or unusual fonts (they do not scan well)

COMPARE

Traditional resumes use active verbs (e.g., developed); scannable resumes use participles (e.g., developing).

A traditional resume format might read:

- Developed promotional materials and brochures
- Created multimedia presentations

Whereas, a scannable resume format might read:

- Graphic designer creating color brochures, multimedia presentations and newspaper ads

Because scannable resumes are not necessarily designed to be attractive, always have a traditional resume on hand. You can add the line "Traditionally formatted resume available upon request" at the bottom of your scannable version.

Other Types of Non-traditional Resumes

In addition to scannable resumes, other non-traditional resume types include:

- The **Electronic resume** (e-resume) can be stored on a computer. You are often asked to fill in a form on screen. Saved as an ASCII or text-only file, text formatting is kept very simple.
- An **E-mail** resume is written in a plain-text application that can then be sent as an attachment or pasted directly into the e-mail message. If an advertisement or recruiter asks for a specific format, such as a Microsoft Word document to be attached to an e-mail message, be sure to follow those instructions exactly.
- The **Web-resume** is published into a website or web page using graphics and hypertext. It is designed to be viewed on a computer monitor.

If you are responding to an employment ad that asks for resumes to be submitted in a specific format, be sure to comply with the format requirements.

Chapter 2

Further Resources and Literature:

Eyler, David. *Resumes that Mean Business*. New York: Random House, 1999.
Fein, Richard. *101 Quick Tips for a Dynamite Resume*. Manassas Park, VA: Impact Publications, 1999
Fry, Ron. *Your First Resume*. Franklin, NJ: Career Press, 2001. This is a very good book for recent graduates.
Messmer, Max. *Job Hunting for Dummies*. IDG Books Worldwide, 1999.
Parker, Yana. *The Resume Catalog: 200 damn Good Examples*. Ten Speed Press. Berkeley, California, 1996.
Weddle, Peter D. *Internet Resumes*. Manassas Park, VA: Impact publications, 1998
Yates, Martin. *Resumes that Knock'em Dead*, Avon, MA: Adams Media Corporation, 2003
Yena, Donna J. *Career Directions*. New York: McGraw-Hill, 1997

The Cover Letter

After your resume, the next important document you need to create is a *cover letter*. A cover letter is a formal letter that accompanies your resume. It is another chance to market yourself. Think of it as a way of introducing yourself to the recruiter. An effective cover letter increases your chances of getting an interview. Without the cover letter, your resume may not even be considered. The letter should be no longer than three-quarters of a page.

Keep in mind that your resume and cover letter create an image of you and your abilities. If these documents do not look professional and are poorly prepared, they will go right into the wastebasket. In the US, it is a common perception that if you cannot represent yourself with professional documents, you are not a desirable employee. And don't be afraid to make positive statements about yourself in your cover letter. Remember, American employers admire self-promotion; they tend to equate it with self-confidence.

In the US, the cover letter follows certain guidelines in format and content. It also should be tailored to the organization and position for which you are applying.

TIP FOR SUCCESS!

Although in many countries employers do not mind a handwritten cover letter, a handwritten cover letter is not acceptable in the US. As with your resume, use standard 8.5"× 11" paper (22cm× 28.5cm). If you are mailing your resume, remember to use matching paper for your resume cover letter and envelope. The most acceptable colors are white, off-white, ivory and light grey.

Cover-Letter Format

The standard cover letter consists of an introduction, body, and a formal closing. Your cover letter should not simply repeat the information in your resume. The body should cover why you are writing, your qualifications, closing information, and refer to your enclosed resume.

TIP FOR SUCCESS

When possible, find out the name and the title of the contact in charge of hiring, and address your cover letter to him or to her. Do not forget to double-check the name. Remember, many people will get annoyed when you misspell or mispronounce their names. You do not want your potential boss to be annoyed with you before you are even called for an interview!

Use the following template and sample cover letter as guides and write your own cover letter:

COVER LETTER TEMPLATE

Introduction:

Return address
Destination address
Date
Salutation (Dear Mr.; Mrs.; Ms.; Dr.; Prof., etc.)

Body:

Paragraph 1: Why you are writing

In the first paragraph state the reason for the letter and reference the source of the job listing. Make sure to mention both the publication title and the date. *Example, "I would like to apply for the position of ESL teacher (or electrical engineer, office manager, nurse, etc.), as advertised in The News Times (or listed on Internet) on November 21, 2006.*

Paragraph 2: Your qualifications

Indicate what you can do for the company and why you are applying for the position. If you have relevant work experience, mention accomplishments related to that position (try not to duplicate information in your resume). If you are a recent college graduate, indicate how your potential employer can benefit from your academic background. Indicate what related work or volunteer experience you have. *Example, "During the past six years I volunteered as an ESL teacher at the community library. In addition, I have created training programs for people who work as volunteers in non-profit organizations. Other related jobs I have held include interpreting for area insurance companies and designing an interpreter manual."*

Paragraph 3: Refer to enclosed resume

Refer to the enclosed resume (and application), which summarizes your qualifications, education and experience. *Example, "The enclosed resume summarizes my experience and qualifications."*

Paragraph 4: Closing paragraph

State that you look forward to hearing from the recruiter, and that you can provide additional information if required. Thank them for taking the time to consider you for the position. *Example, "I look forward to hearing from you. Thank you for your consideration."* You can also add *"I will follow up with a phone call in a few days."*

Formal Closing:

"Sincerely yours", or "Yours truly"

Your signature

Your name (typed)

Chapter 2

A Basic Cover Letter Sample

> Peter Italiano
> 55 Mill Drive
> Small Town, New York
>
> January 20, 2007
>
> December 14, 2007
>
> John Vanelli
> All-American Company
> US city, State, USA
>
> Dear Mr. John Vanelli:
>
> I am writing in response to your advertisement for an Italian language translator in The News Times dated November 18, 2006.
>
> As outlined in the accompanying resume, I have a background that precisely matches the job requirements described in your ad. I have one year of job experience in the field, having been employed as an interpreter and translator for Milano clothing company in New York City. In this position, I have interpreted for negotiations concerning apparel design, and translated agreements, garment descriptions, and correspondence.
>
> I am open to relocation and would enjoy working in Los Angeles. I look forward to hearing from you.
>
> Sincerely,
>
> *Peter Italiano (Signature)*
>
> Peter Italiano (Name typed)
>
> Enclosure

Additional Cover Letter Resources and Literature:

Besson, Taunee s. *Cover Letters.* John Wiley & Sons. Canada, 1999.
Block A., Jay, CPRW, Betrus, Michael, CPRW. *101 Best Cover Letters.* New York: McGraw-Hill, 1999

Yates, Martin. *Cover Letters That Knock 'em Dead*. Holbrook, MA: Adams Media Corporation, 2003
Wynett, Stanley. *Cover letters that will get you job you want*. Cincinnati, OH: Better way books, 1989.

Educational Credentials and Licensing

If you are educated outside the US, you may need to prove that your education is equivalent to American standards. Many job recruiters do not ask you to present a copy of your degree. Nevertheless, it is essential to have official documents available in case you are asked to present them.

To determine how your educational credentials compare to American standards, you need to have your credentials evaluated. In the following paragraphs, we discuss how to go about it. At the interview be prepared to present your education in terminology understandable to the American employers.

NOTE!

Most American employers will only understand your diplomas or other credentials if you provide the American equivalents. For this reason you need to evaluate your educational documents in terms understood by American employers, educational institutions, licensing and certification boards.

Certain jobs in the US require licensing. See below for guidance in obtaining licenses for your particular profession or job interest.

Licensing
1. *Some professions (for example, medical) require licensing. Contact your state licensing board to find out about the exam you need to take to get a license.*
2. *Professional Licensing is a government or industrial certification stating that an individual is professionally qualified according to the standards of that country. For example, medical doctors licensed outside the United States must complete the licensing process in America in order to practice medicine in that country.*
3. *Job seekers would need to have license in place **before** starting interview process. However, Martin Yates advises to list the information about the status of your accreditation or licensing (e.g. past all parts of CPA exam, date, expected certification, date) even before you receive the document.*
4. *To find a state Licensing Board for a given profession, go on-line. Go to search engine, www.Google.com, type in the state and profession in question, for instance," Connecticut Medical Licensing". Medical Licensing Agencies by state are listed at www.dcmonline.org/practicerelocation/licencing.agencies.htm.*

Evaluating Your Credentials – What you Need and Where to Go

In the US, private organizations and some universities perform credential evaluations. At the end of this section, you can find a list of selected reputable resources.

In order to have your credentials evaluated, you will need the following items:

1. **Clear photocopies** (diplomas, academic records, etc.). Make sure that all stamps and signatures are visible. Sometimes the evaluating organization will request the original documents for verification. Make sure that you mail them using a reliable mail carrier.

2. **English translation.** You will need a word-for-word English translation of your documentation. The translation can be done in your own country or in the US. In some cases, the employers request a notarized translation; so make sure to notarize the translated documents.

There are two basic evaluation types available:

1. **Document-by-Document** – contains a description of your credentials (name, major field of study, US equivalent)

2. **Course-by-Course** – contains all the above, plus a summary of all subjects studied and courses taken, and an analysis of the US credit and grade equivalent for each course.

Generally, for employment, you will need a document-by-document evaluation, and to pursue professional licensing or to continue education you will need a course-by-course evaluation.

Selected credential evaluation resources

www.cedevaluations.com – Center for Educational Documentation, (617) 338-7171
www.naces.org – National Association of Credential Evaluation Services lists an extensive number of agencies evaluating foreign educational credentials in this country.
www.ece.org – Educational Credential Evaluators, Inc., a non-profit public service organization. Contact jimfrey@ece.org or (414) 289-3400.
www.wes.org - World Education Services.1-800-937-3895, (212) 966-6311

The Application Form

Usually, a potential employer will require you to fill out an employer-specific application form in addition to submitting your resume. The application form generally assists the employer's Human Resources/Employment Department administrators in collecting common information from all applicants. Very often you will be asked to fill out the application form paperwork in the employer's office. As a rule, an application form will require basic information such as:

- Your name, address, telephone number, social security number
- Dates of previous jobs, names and addresses of previous employers
- Dates of schooling, degrees or certifications held, and names of educational institutions
- Your eligibility to work in the US.

Make sure that you write the information neatly. If your application does not make a good impression, it could hinder your chances with that employer. In fact, for some lower-end jobs, a resume is neither required nor requested; instead, only a completed job application form is required.

In addition to an application form, you may be asked by some employers to complete a test related to your personal qualities and qualifications. CVS Pharmacy, a national chain of drug stores, has the job applicants take an on-line test. One of the goals of the test is to evaluate how the applicant would deal with the customers and co-workers.

Moving On

In this chapter we discussed the importance of creating a professional resume, cover letter, and other supporting documentation. If you have assembled the documents outlined in this chapter, then you have completed Step 1. Now it's time to move on to Step 2 — the search for job openings.

Chapter Glossary

Buzzword: a job-relevant word or term on a resume aimed at catching the attention of the reader (recruiter); a key word

Credentials: degrees, certifications, training

Cover letter: letter that accompanies your resume

Chronological resume: a resume in which you list your experience in chronological order (starting with the most recent and working your way back in time)

Combination resume: resume that groups your skills and experiences within specific sets

Relocation: moving from one place to another

Format: way to organize information

Functional resume: lists the skills with supporting achievements, placing emphasis on your abilities rather than time, place and order in which you achieved your skills

Hire: to employ

Key word: an industry term, a buzzword

Professional licensing: a government or industrial certification that an individual is qualified according to the standards of a given country

References: the people who can be contacted to confirm the information you have in your resume or vouch for you as an employee and a person

Scannable resume: a resume that can be scanned into a computer

Skill: ability, talent, proficiency

Toll-free: no-charge (free) telephone call

Traditional resume: a standard paper resume that you will mail or fax to the employer

Transferable (skills): skills that can be applied in many areas

Chapter 3

Step 2: FIND JOB OPENINGS

In this Chapter: ●Employment information resources ● Professions in demand in the US — where to start ● Classified ads in the newspaper ● Executive search firms (headhunters) ● Employment agencies ● The Internet ● Networking ● Four easy steps for effective networking ● Networking events ● Moving on ● Chapter glossary

> *"There are always vacancies...Organizations are born,... expand, ...workers quit,*
> *change jobs, or become handicapped, retire, or die."*
> *Richard Bolles, best selling author of What Color is Your Parachute?*

Employment Information Resources

In Chapter 2 you learned how to produce the professional resume and other documents needed to market yourself in America. The next step is to find what job openings exist. How *do* people find jobs in the US? In this chapter we explore ways to locate job opportunities and offer tips for success.

If you are currently in the US, you can find job opportunities by:

- reading job postings in local newspapers
- searching for job listings on the Internet
- contacting employment agencies and executive recruiters
- networking with (talking to) people you know

Other resources include professional publications, job fairs, personnel/human resources offices of companies, college placement services, and state employment offices. Note, however, that state employment offices service primarily citizens or permanent residents (permanent residents are those who have a green card).

One of the best ways to find out about potential job openings is through *networking*. As we will explain in more detail in this chapter and in Chapter 8, networking is the process of building connections with a variety of people by establishing relationships with the people you meet. The more connections (or contacts) you make, the greater is the probability that one of those contacts is a potential employer. As you can see, it is to your advantage to network with everyone you know and meet— your friends and family, your doctor, and even the people at your neighborhood café, diner or restaurant! In other words, network with *everyone*! In this chapter we will discuss how to network as well as networking etiquette appropriate to the US culture.

In the sections that follow, we will first look at professions in demand in the US and then explore in greater detail each of the resources available for finding the job listings that interest you.

Professions in Demand in the US — Where to Start

The United States is the wealthiest country in the world, with a dynamic, flexible, and mobile workforce. It is also the most popular destination in the world.

Despite occasional downturns, the US has a strong, dynamic, flexible and vibrant economy. Specialists predict that in the coming years there will be an increasing demand for skilled workers to maintain that economy. Although job opportunities vary by field at any given time, and some American industries have moved their operations overseas, the current population will not be sufficient to meet the manpower demands. This means that there will be plenty of job opportunities for immigrants and foreign nationals.

How can you find out what professions are in demand at any given time? From the following resources, you can learn which professions are in demand:

1. Networking with individuals employed in the same or similar industries

2. Mass media — newspapers, television, radio and the Internet

3. Employment agencies and executive recruiters (headhunters)

4. Professional associations in your field

5. US Government websites (such as BLS – Bureau of Labor Statistics, http://www.bls.gov/oco/ or DOL – Department of Labor, http://www.doleta.gov/jobseekers/).

Industries such as the hospitality industry (hotels and restaurants), healthcare (hospitals and doctors' offices) and information technology (programming, networks and computers) currently have the greatest need for foreign labor. Specialists predict that the shortage will increase in the years to come. According to www.careervoyages.gov, the economy is expected to continue creating jobs for workers at all levels of education and training. Occupations that require vocational certification or a college degree are estimated to have faster growth rates than occupations requiring less education and training. *The President's High Growth Job Training Initiative* identified 12 sectors of the economy in which skilled workers will be needed. These sectors are:

- Advanced Manufacturing
- Aerospace
- Automotive
- Biotechnology
- Energy
- Financial Services
- Geospacial Technology
- Healthcare
- Hospitality
- Information Technology
- Retail
- Transportation

Does this mean that there are no opportunities for other professions? Not at all. It only means that some jobs are easier to find than others.

The hospitality industry is one sector in which work is relatively easy to find. Jobs requiring less skill, education, and experience — such as hotel and restaurant service and maintenance positions — are usually in demand. These jobs are often advertised in shop windows or inside restaurants and hotels. You may want to take one of these jobs to pay your bills while you are looking for a better position in your field, or while you are going to school or are in training. The hospitality industry is one of the fastest growing industries in the US. Should you take a temporary job in hospitality, and discover you like it, you can pursue a career in the field by earning a college degree.

Your native language can be an asset to you in finding a job. If you are from a Spanish speaking country with a background in teaching, you may be able to find work as a bilingual educator.

Another way to capitalize on your foreign language capabilities is to freelance as an interpreter. Many companies and organizations use agencies specializing in interpreting to help them communicate with the non-English speaking customers. If you qualify to be an interpreter, you can often work part-time from home during hours that are convenient for you. Check the web for tele-interpreters. There are scores of companies providing phone and on-site interpreting, and demand for this service in the US and globally is growing. Here are a couple companies to check out.

- *Network OMNI* – a multilingual communication company, provides interpreters in various fields and languages; 1-800-893-6650, 1-800-700-2335.
- *Tele-interpreters on Call* – same as above, 1-877- 641-1411, 1-800-338-5811.

If you are looking for a teaching position, visit www.recruitingteachers.org to get information on National *Teacher Recruitment Clearinghouse* – an organization devoted to teacher recruitment nationwide; (617) 489-6000. Teaching positions are widely advertised in local newspapers as well.

Chapter 3

The healthcare arena is another area high in demand. If you are a skilled nurse or nurse's assistant, have working knowledge of English, and meet certain qualification criteria you can be hired immediately.

Medical support people are urgently needed throughout the US. Many colleges and universities offer educational opportunities in healthcare. You can find their list in the directory at the end of this book.

Healthcare recruiting is prevalent on the Internet. The following is a list of resources.

> www.medhunters.com; www.nationjob.com/medical; www.healthcaresource.com;
> www.jobscience.com; www.medicalworkers.com; www.medzilla.com;
> www.healthcareerweb.com

Nursing professionals are in high demand in the US. This demand is going to increase due to aging of the American population. Nurses from foreign countries must take the CFGNS exam before they can be certified to practice in the US. If you go on line and type in "CGFNS" you can reach the website www.cgfns.org. The website describes the certification process and what is needed to work as a nurse in the US.

TIP FOR SUCCESS!

If you don't find the job you want right away, accept a lower paying job that will help pay your bills. Then build your professional skills as a volunteer in a non-profit organization and join a professional association in your field.

NOTE

The above-mentioned tip for success does not apply to all professions. For example, a doctor from another country can't volunteer in a non-profit health clinic to "build professional skills"; s/he might volunteer in a non-professional capacity to become familiar with the American practice of medicine through observation. The same might be said of an immigrating lawyer, nurse or any professional who might need to be re-licensed in the US.

The US government is the largest employer in the US. Http://www.usajobs.opm.gov lists a great variety of job openings throughout the country. Explore thousands of jobs on the USAJOBS database.

NOTE

As a rule, you need to be a US citizen to qualify for government jobs. However, federal agencies are permitted to hire non-citizens when there are no qualified citizens available.

Libraries can help you at all stages of your job search.

Public Libraries
Public libraries in the US are powerful information clearing houses. They can be invaluable to your job search. They are a great source of information about companies that are expanding and hiring. If you know your way around the library, you will save countless hours of time and frustration. Many libraries cater to the special needs of immigrants and foreign nationals. Many are becoming more and more a source of education.
Librarians can be particularly helpful in your job quest. Look in the "jobs and careers" section and ask a librarian to help you. To get an overview of a particular industry and details about companies, consider using *Standard and Poor's* directory. The annual subscription to this publication is quite expensive, but many libraries have it available for

> public use.
>
> Many libraries hire trainers to conduct employability courses. I have conducted many seminars on *How to Get a Job in the US* in Connecticut and New York libraries.

If you are outside the US and looking for a job in the US, the Internet is a great place to start. Many companies post open positions on their websites. The Internet can also help you find a job with an American company outside the US. Companies like Kodak, General Electric and others have divisions throughout the world.

You can find lots of international nonprofit employers as well.

To find the best companies for you, try visiting the following websites:

www.fortune.com – Fortune magazine posts company rankings such as *Global 500, Global Most Admired*, and *50 Best for Minorities*.

www.forbes.com/lists – Forbes magazine posts similar company lists such as *Forbes 500, Global 2000*, and *200 Best Small Companies*. There is also a *2003 Job Benefits Survey*, which shows what benefits (insurance, 401K, etc.) America's 300 largest companies are offering. (To get access to this information you need to subscribe to Fortune magazine.)

www.workingmother.com/100best.shtml – *Working Mother Magazine* shows the 100 best companies for women based on family benefits.

www.aarp.org/bestemployers/ – My *Generation*, the AARP magazine, lists the best employers for people over 50 years old.

www.latinastyle.com/latina50.html – *Latina Style* magazine offers a list of the 50 best employers for Hispanic women.

www.computerworld.com/departments – *Computerworld* magazine publishes an annual list of the top 100 companies for Information Technology (IT) professionals.

www.aifs.com – *American* Institute for Foreign Study *(AIFS)* sends au pairs (live-in homecare workers, maids, babysitters) to the US and worldwide; in the US tel.: 1-800-727-AIFS; outside the US (203) 399-5000. They are working predominantly with high school students.

www.idealist.org – A directory of non-profits all over the world. The browser will find organizations by mission statement, topic or geographical location.

www.cci-exchange.com – The Center for Cultural Interchange (CCI) provides work and travel or internship opportunities for college students in the United States. They work through agencies in countries all over the world.

www.nonprofitexpert.com – When you select "Resource Links" from the menu on this website, you will find an extensive list of links to non-profit organizations around the globe.

Classified Ads in the Newspaper

Newspapers are the most common source of job openings or employment for jobs requiring little or no previous experience, as well as for lower and middle management jobs. Most newspapers have an employment section every Sunday. Some larger papers have job ads every day or several days a week.

Today, many national and local newspapers have on-line editions (for example, www.washingtonpost.com and www.nytimes.com) enabling you to view their employment classifieds via the Internet. With the help of your computer, you can find a job opening from anywhere in the world without buying a hard copy of the newspaper.

NOTE
Note, however, that for those who are not citizens or have no immigrant visas, it is almost impossible to be legally employed, even in lower-end jobs, without special BCIS (Bureau of Citizenship and Immigration Service) permission.

Executive Search Firms (Headhunters)

A "headhunter" is a recruiter who matches senior-level professionals to executive positions. Companies that employ headhunters are generally called "executive search firms." In most cases, employers pay the recruiter to find them a suitable candidate — which means that you most likely won't have to pay for this service. Headhunters will do a background check to make sure that you qualify for a high-level position before referring you to their clients. You can find advertisements for headhunters in large national newspapers such as the Washington Post or New York Times.

Working with headhunters is a great way to learn more about job searching in the US. You can learn a lot from speaking with skilled headhunters. They can offer you insider tips about your industry — such as salary information — and can be a valuable career adviser.

Most headhunters specialize in a particular field, such as biotechnology, accounting, sales, software engineering, fashion, etc. Make sure that you are choosing a headhunting firm that specializes in your field. Also find out whether the firm earns its compensation from employers or from job candidates. Most search firms do not charge the candidate for their services.

To register with a headhunter, you can send your resume along with a cover letter similar to the example below. You can also send information in the form of an e-mail (See the guidelines on e-mail writing in Chapter 8). Remember to mention in the letter or e-mail your salary requirements and whether you are willing to relocate.

A Sample Letter to an Executive Search Firm

January 20, 2007

Yanek Kotowski
Your address
Your phone number

Mr. Ken Sutherland
Headhunting Firm
Street Address, City, State USA

Dear Mr. Sutherland:

I am forwarding my resume because I understand you specialize in placing clients in the biomechanical field.

I am hoping that you have one or two clients who may be looking for someone with my qualifications. I am currently earning the equivalent of 55K USD per year. My permanent address is in Poland: I am, of course, open to relocation.

I have enclosed my resume for your review. I can be reached at ... Phone Number and/or e-mail address.

I look forward to hearing from you.

Sincerely,

Your name typed under signature

Enclosures

Employment Agencies

Headhunters are most likely to be interested in working with you if you are looking for a salary above the $50,000 range. If your target salary range is lower than that, your best bet would be an employment agency. Check in advance if you are required to pay a fee for their services. When an agency states in their ad "fee paid," it means that the employer (not you, the applicant) pays for the agency's services. You can find employment agencies on the Internet (www.SmartPages.com) and in your local commercial phonebook (e.g., Yellow Pages).

The Internet

The Internet has become a popular source for job listings. According to Richard Bolles, the author of the bestselling job-hunting classic, there are thousands of Internet sites devoted to job search. The largest, very popular portal is Monster.com. Other examples of career and job related sites are Careermozaics.com, Flipdog.com, CareerBuilder.com, Jobs.com and Hotjobs.com.

The US Government is a major employer. You can find information on government job openings and employment counseling services at *usajobs.opm.gov*. The website www.statejobs.com lists links to employment opportunities and services in all 50 states.

Most of these sites are designed to be intuitive and easy to navigate; a good website will walk you through the process. To find these websites, visit a search engine such as Google.com or Dogpile.com, and type in "Job Search in the US" or "Employment in the US." Keep trying different search engines. You may find some new sites. I personally like Richard Bolles's website (www.tenspeed.com/parachute), which has a section on searching for jobs. Another excellent resource is http://careers.msn.com, which is supported by MSN together with CareerBuilder. It not only gives you an opportunity to search for jobs but features useful information on careers and jobs.

A very useful book for job seekers is *Weddle's Directory of Employment Related Internet sites*. This comprehensive directory lists sites by their name in one of three categories: occupational field, industry and specialty.

Many companies post job openings on their websites. Therefore an excellent way to find job openings is to go directly to the targeted company's website and submit your resume as instructed.

Useful Resources and Literature:

www.usajobs.opm.gov – the US Government's official site for jobs and hiring information. It features a bank of thousands of jobs. As a rule, you need to be a citizen to qualify for government jobs. However, federal agencies are permitted to hire non-citizens when there are no qualified citizens available.
www.monster.com – a one-stop career management resource, job search, resume management
www.hotjobs.com – provides on-line recruiting solutions for employers and job seekers
www.CareerBuilder.com – the site allows searching for jobs in many major cities throughout the US
Weddle's Directory of Employment Related Sites, 2005. Check updates on Weddles.com.

Chapter 3

Networking

"People aren't strangers if you have already met them.
The trick is to meet them before you need them."
Harvey Mackey, American networking guru

Any source of employment listings can potentially lead to a job but, statistically, networking is by far the most probable way to find a job (about 85-90% of jobs are found through networking). That is why I recommend making networking a priority. Effective networking is a skill that you may need to learn.

STATISTIC

According to the US Department of Labor, 10-15% of job openings are "visible" the rest are "invisible." 85-90% of job openings are found through networking. This means that networking is the most effective way of finding a job in the US.

Learning to make useful contacts, American-style, can be one of the most powerful tools in obtaining satisfactory employment in the US. However, you should know the rules because it can challenge the way that you are used to doing things in your country of origin.

What is networking? Networking is *the process* of making contacts or looking for information for professional purposes by making contacts. In other words, networking is an informal way of getting a job or information about a job opening through interacting with people.

What is a network? A network is *a group of people* who have something in common and/or come together on a regular basis; for instance, family and friends, a professional association, a club, people attending the same church or place of worship. Your network is the people who you know.

You should maintain your network whether you have a job or not. According to networking guru Harvey Mackey, "People aren't strangers if you have already met them. The trick is to meet them before you need them."

When looking for employment, networking is not just about contacting people you know and asking them for a job. It is not asking for a job directly; it is asking for information leading to an employment opportunity.

TIP FOR
SUCCESS!

Since most jobs in the US are found through networking, the ability to network in this country is essential to every job seeker. It is not merely an important way of finding your perfect job. It will increase the possibility of finding friends and acquaintances with similar interests. Networking can lead to a better quality of life by meeting interesting people and new friends.

There are many countries in which people find jobs through networking with people they know. However, in the US, you can often find employment by contacting *people who you have never met before* — provided you know the rules. Although building a network in the US takes time and persistence, it leads to results much more quickly (or more readily) than it would in other countries. For this reason, you must take advantage of this effective tool when searching for work here.

COMPARE

1. *In the US, unlike many other countries, you can often find employment by contacting people who you have never met before – but you should know the rules of networking.*

2. *Most employers, especially those who have not previously hired foreign born, are more likely to consider you if you were referred by someone who they trust.*

3. *To network effectively in the US you need to apply certain rules of etiquette, which may be different from the way things are typically done in your country.*

Learning to network American-style will increase your chances of being hired or, conversely, decrease the possibility of being rejected. In the next section, we explain the right way to network in the US.

Four Easy Steps for Effective Networking

Before engaging in any networking activities, learn the four steps involved in networking:

Step 1: Develop networking tools such as a networking list and self-presentation.

Step 2: Set up goals for yourself. For instance, your goal may be to make two contacts at an event; one may become a good job referral, another may become a good friend or acquaintance with interests similar to yours.

Step 3: Attend networking events such as social or professional gatherings.

Step 4: Follow up on new contacts with notes, phone calls, or e-mail. Remember, following up will considerably increase the probability of your success.

Now, let's look at each step in more detail.

Step 1: Develop Networking Tools

Developing networking tools, such as your contact list and self-presentation, and learning how to use them can go a long way in getting a job. Let's look at each of these.

A. Your Contact List. Put together a list of people who might be able to help you find employment. You may use the worksheet on the next page. It will help you develop a list of names and contact information for the various categories of people with whom you regularly interact. If needed, use more space for each category. Depending on your situation, you might not have all the following categories in place (for instance, if you are not religious and do not visit a place of worship, you will not have category two and three as part of your network). Generally speaking, your contacts fall under two categories, personal and professional.

Fill out the relevant information in the worksheet and you will have your first networking list. Keep in mind that this is a general list of potential contacts. You might not have all the categories filled. On the other hand, you should take time to think about any additional groups of people who may influence the success of your job search.

Chapter 3

Your Contact List Worksheet
(Add space whenever necessary)

PERSONAL CONTACTS

1. Your family (parents, grandparents, sisters, brothers, cousins, aunts, uncles and their friends and extended family)

_____

2. Your friends and friends of their friends and relatives

_____

2. Your priest, minister, molla, rabbi, poojari, lama, etc.

_____

3. Members of your house of worship (church, temple, synagogue, mosque, etc.)

_____

4. Your teachers

_____

5. Your neighbors

_____

PROFESSIONAL CONTACTS

1. Professionals you buy services from (Your doctor, lawyer, banker or financial advisor, your insurance agent, mechanic/car dealer, etc.)

_____

2. Present and past co-workers

_____

3. Customers and clients

_____

4. School alumni

_____

OTHER CATEGORIES (people you work out in the gym with, professional association members, your club members, etc.)

_____

This list is just a start. Now you need to maintain and develop your network. As you meet people at parties, conventions, in your church or temple, or any sort of gathering, replenish your list with people you meet. Keep your contact list on a Rolodex or electronic database.

B. Self-presentation. Now that you have compiled your contact list, it is time to develop and practice another important tool: your self-presentation.

A self-presentation in America is the way you introduce yourself to others and it is often called your "sales pitch" (remember self-marketing?). It may last anywhere from a few seconds to a minute. The goal of self-presentation is to grab the attention of your contact and provide basic, relevant information about you and your skills. It should be short, clear, and relevant. You should develop several variations of your self-presentations to use in different settings. For instance, develop a self-presentation for a business event (for instance, association meeting) and another for social gatherings (a wedding party or a birthday).

Listed below are some examples of simple self-presentations. In Chapter 8 you will find a short worksheet to help you customize one for yourself.

1. *Hi! I am _____. Or: My name is Juana. I am a photographer. I specialize in family portraits.*

2. *Hi, my name is_____. I'm a secretary in a real estate firm. I organize property listings and update client files.* Then depending on the situation, you may use a little more detail here, for example, *"I am the sister of the hostess".*

3. *Hello! My name is_____. I am an interpreter. I help people from different countries understand each other.*

Then to continue the conversation, you may say *"And what do you do?"* or "Are you a member of this organization?" or *"How do you know the hosts?"*

To create your own self-presentation and learn more about it and other networking and job search tools, read Chapter 8. It contains in-depth information about self-presentation and other networking tools such as small talk (which means casual not-business related conversation), working the room (networking with people in the room) and thank you/follow up letters and notes.

Step 2: Set up Goals

Before attending any networking event, set up your goals by writing down what you want to achieve at that event. Use the following sheet for setting up your goals.

TIP FOR SUCCESS!

Remember, setting up goals will considerably increase your chances of success. It is true in any type of endeavor, and your job search in the US is not an exception.

1._____

    For example, "have a conversation with three interesting people."

2._____

    For example, "Find two potential friends or contacts."

3._____

For example, "Find three potential (job information) leads."

TIP FOR SUCCESS!

To keep focused on your goals, write them down. Keep them on your desk or somewhere visible.

Step 3: Attend Networking Events

Now that you have your self-presentation and goals in place, it is time to get down to business – attending networking events. You can meet your contacts practically anywhere: parties, weddings, places of worship, volunteering, seminars, health clubs, professional associations, even waiting in line in the DMV (Department of Motor Vehicles) when registering your car or getting your driver's license.

TIP FOR SUCCESS!

Do not forget setting up your goals before you attend networking events. Decide in advance what you want to accomplish at the event. Most importantly, enjoy being at the events and meeting new people and seeing again old acquaintances and friends!

Step 4: Follow up

Always follow up after networking events. If somebody promised you valuable information, call that person and politely remind him/her about the promise. Say *"Hi, how are you? (or I hope you are well). Just a quick follow up. Did you have a chance to look up the information for me? (Did you have a chance to speak to… about…?). I am calling to follow up on information that we talked about…"*

Your contact may introduce you to others, refer you to someone who may know about job openings, give feedback on your resume or suggest organizations that you might join. Whatever advice or help your contacts offers be sure to thank them for their time and effort. See a sample of a thank you letter in Chapter 8, *Letters.* Send each person a thank you letter or an e-mail. Or better yet, mail a thank you card with your words of appreciation.

NOTE!

You can buy a thank you card in many stores in the US. Check out a sample of multilingual thank-you card at **www.SucceedinAmerica.com**.

Next, let's review networking events.

Networking Events

The Networking Interview. One of the most effective ways of making professional contacts is the networking interview, also referred to as an informational or exploratory interview. See more about this kind of interview in Chapter 4, *Interview Types.*

The networking interview is different from a formal job interview. In Chapter 8's *Working the Room* and *Networking Conversation* you will find more on how to set up a networking interview by phone after a networking event or when you are referred by a friend.

COMPARE

The basic difference between a formal job interview and an informational interview is that you are not asking for a job, but for information about a job, company and the industry in general. The purpose of the informational interview is to learn more about your career field and to expand your network.

Here are some questions you may want to ask during the informational interview

- Is my resume appropriate for someone seeking a job in this field?
- What aspects of your job do you find most interesting?
- What aspects do you enjoy least?
- How did you get your current job?
- What training programs or classes will help me?
- What volunteer experiences would increase my chances of finding a job in my field?
- What is the salary range in the field?
- Will you let me know if you hear of any job openings that fit my qualifications and experience?
- Who would you recommend that I contact next?

TIP FOR SUCCESS!

Never leave the exploratory interview without asking the following question: Can you suggest someone else in the field whom I may contact? If the answer is yes, it will help you to expand your network and may lead you to a job opening.

Joining Clubs/Organizations and Volunteering

A great way of meeting people and making friends is by joining professional or social organizations. The best ones for meeting friends are those that meet regularly and often. Here are some tips on how to make the most of joining clubs and volunteering.

- Be active in an organization and join committees or volunteer.
- Keep in mind that sometimes it takes a year or so to develop a close relationship. Friendships and business relationships often form naturally, but they do not happen overnight.
- If for some reason one club or organization does not work for you, try another.
- Be aware that there are sometimes fees or membership dues related to participating in professional organizations.
- To find an association in your field you can:
  1. Search on-line
  2. Visit your local library and check out the "Encyclopedia of Associations" published by Gale Research
  3. Talk to people who are employed in the target industry.

A good way to find organizations for which to volunteer is to visit the web. Here are three websites you can use to get information.

www.VolunteerMatch.com – you can find thousands of volunteer opportunities on this website, sorted by geographical location, field of interest, or organization name.

www.idealist.org – This is a directory of non-profits all over the world. The browser will find organizations by mission statement, topic or geographical location.

www.nonprofitexpert.com – when you select "Resource Links" from the menu on this website, you will find an extensive list of links to non-profit organizations around the globe.

Let's summarize the key actions to establish and maintain an effective network:

1. Create your self-presentation
2. Develop and rehearse variations of self-presentations
3. Continue updating your networking list
4. Practice self-presentation
5. Compile a list of networking events
6. Schedule your networking
7. Set up goals before each event
8. Keep records of your contacts
9. Cultivate and expand your network
10. Follow up, follow up, follow up

Moving On

We talked about the basics of networking in this chapter. In *Chapter 8*, you will find additional information on networking such as *Networking Over the Phone*, *Working the Room* and other networking related topics.

And now, if you have your resume and documents in place (*Chapter 2*, Step 1) and know how to look for jobs (*Chapter 3*, Step 2), it is time to move on to *Chapter 4*, Step 3 – Preparing for an Interview!

Further Resources and Literature

Bolles, Richard. *What color is your parachute? A Practical Guide for Job-Hunters and Career Changers.* 2005 edition, revised annually, 8 million copies in print, in 12 languages. Ten Speed Press, Berkeley, CA. *Encyclopedia of Associations.* Gale Research, 1975 – current year.
Glass, Ph.D, Lilian. *Say it right. How to talk in any social situation. Harper Collins Publishers, Inc., 1990.*
Mackay, Harvey. *Dig your well before you're thirsty.* The only networking book you'll ever need. New York, 1997
Richardson, Douglas B. *Networking.* John Wiley & Sons, 1994
www.VolunteerMatch.com – website for volunteer opportunity for "whatever you like doing" in the U.S.

Chapter Glossary

Alumni: graduates, former students, old pupils
Au Pair: a foreigner, usually a young person, who lives in a family and helps to take care of children in exchange for room and board
BCIS (formerly INS) – Bureau of Citizenship and Immigration Service
Bilingual: able to speak two languages
Employment agency: firm in the business of placing people in jobs
Executive search firm (*syn* headhunting firm*):* firms specializing in placing senior managers and executives in jobs
Freelance: to perform work for more than one party or organization without being committed to a single employer
Global: worldwide, encompassing all countries and continents
Headhunter: an executive recruiter
Help wanted ad: job advertisement in a newspaper
Hospitality industry: hotel/motel industry
INS: Immigration and Naturalization Service, the US Government agency that controls visas and entries into the US
Job posting: information about a job opening (usually in a newspaper or internally in the company)
Lower-end job: low-paying job
Networking: the process of exchanging information with people of similar interests for professional purposes
Networking list: List of contacts with details (phone number, address, title, etc.)
Networking tools: information necessary to initiate and conduct effective networking
Networking interview: an interview with a professional in your field that helps you build knowledge about an industry, company, contacts and job openings
Non-profit: describes an organization operating not for profit (but for common good)
Permanent Resident Visa: a document permitting an individual to live and work in the US for an unlimited period of time (otherwise known as a "Green Card")
Place (*verb*): find an employment opportunity (agencies place applicants in jobs)

Pitch (sales pitch): see: self-presentation
Multinational: transnational, international, worldwide
Search engine: Web-based tool that enables you to locate specific websites.
Self-presentation (*syn* sales pitch, a commercial): brief, relevant description of oneself
Skill: ability, talent
Tutoring: teaching, training, coaching
Volunteering: working without being paid (usually for a non-profit organization)
Word of mouth: conversationally, orally
Work the room: network with everyone in the room
Yellow Pages: a local commercial phone book

Chapter 4

Step 3: PREPARE FOR THE INTERVIEW

> *"The will to win is important, but the will to prepare is vital"*
> Joe Paterno, an American coach of college football

In this Chapter: ● The importance of the interview ● Pre-interview company research ● Understand job requirements ● What to bring ● How to dress and groom ● Preparing for common interview questions ● Preparing your own questions ● Handling immigration status questions ● Diversity in the workplace and you ●Practicing the interview ● Interview practice scorecard ● Interview types ● Moving on ● Chapter glossary

The Importance of the Interview

Every road to employment in the US goes through the job interview. What is a job interview? Simply put, it is a conversation, a dialogue during which the job applicant convinces the employer that he or she can fulfill the job requirements, solve problems for the employer, and, most importantly, is the best candidate for the job.

Why is the interview such an important stage in the hiring process? In the United States, employers use the interview to screen job applicants and ultimately to select the person they feel is the best person for the job. The best candidate, however, is not necessarily the one with the best qualifications. Even if you have excellent professional skills and a perfect resume, you will not win the position unless you can convince the interviewer that you are the best person for the job. Thus your self-presentation skills become equally, if not more, important than your qualifications in determining whether you are offered a job.

Most employers do not make a final hiring decision after the first interview. Instead, after all candidates have had an initial interview, the employer typically selects two or more candidates for a second interview and eliminates the rest, those whose interview performance was clearly inferior to the others. After the round two interviews, the employer either decides who gets the job offer or, if necessary, goes to a third round of interviews to further evaluate the finalists for the job. Now you can see the more skilled you are in your self-presentation, the more confidently you present yourself, and the more prepared you are for the interview, the greater the chance you have of landing that job!

NOTE!   *At the interview, your goal is to get a job offer or, at least, get to a second interview.*

Now that we've established the importance of the interview, let's analyze the it in detail and see what we can do to prepare ourselves for it.

An interview can either be conducted in person or "off-site" with the help of media (by phone, on the Web, or through video-conferencing). To better understand the interview process, let's look at it from the employer's perspective. Normally the employer goes through four preliminary steps when searching for new hires:

1. Advertising the job opening and receiving resumes in reply

2. Reviewing the resumes and selecting candidates whom they think best match the job requirements

3. Conducting a preliminary screening of selected candidates

4. Selecting the candidates for the final interviews.

In many ways, the interview is a test. Most people who apply for the job will the have the minimum required qualifications. To win the job, you will need to stand out from the competition. Yet, you won't necessarily need to be the best or the brightest "on paper" — you simply need to market yourself more effectively than the rest. In this chapter we will help you to prepare for your interview so that you can present yourself to the employer as the best candidate for the job. Preparing ahead of time will ensure your confidence and improve your chance of success. It takes just a few steps to prepare for an interview:

- Conduct pre-interview research
- Understand job requirements
- Know what to bring to the interview
- Know how to dress and groom yourself
- Prepare to answer typical questions
- Compile your own questions
- Practice the interview

In the sections that follow, we take you through each of these key steps.

Pre-interview Company Research

Acquiring some basic knowledge about the company or organization for which you hope to work is the first step in preparing for your interview.

What information should you look for? Knowing the following specific information will aid your cause during the interview:

- Company products and/or services
- Name and background of the company leader
- Company culture[4] (the best way to do that is to speak to the individuals currently employed by the organization)
- Terminology and expressions commonly used in the industry and company
- The different divisions the company has and where they are located
- The prospects of growth and recent reorganizations or mergers
- Recent awards or other events that might have been mentioned in the media or as press releases.

The more basic knowledge you have about an employer the better you can converse with, and therefore impress, the interviewer.

Where should you look for information? The fastest and easiest way to track down all of this information is by going to the company's website. If you don't know the Web address, try typing the company name into the search engine Google.com or any search engine you might be comfortable using. If the company doesn't have a website, or if the site does not offer useful information, you can also try visiting business information websites such as hoovers.com or businessweek.com. These and similar sites will provide you with accurate, unbiased information. Other sources include:

1. For large companies,
   - *The U.S. Bureau of Labor Statistics at http://stats.bls.gov.*

---

[4] Company culture is how things are done there – hierarchy, management style, attitude to tardiness/absenteeism, telecommuting, flexibility, etc.

- *The following resources are available in many US public libraries:*
  - o *Standard and Poor's Register of Corporations, Directors and Executives (Standard and Poors, New York, NY)*
  - o *Thomas Register of American Manufacturers (Thomas Publishing Company, New York, NY)*

2. For smaller companies,

- Contact trade associations or your local Chamber of Commerce.
- Look for employee handbooks, annual reports, and sales/marketing brochures. Annual reports are also called 10-K reports and found in many libraries.
- Check the Better Business Bureau's website to see whether there have been complaints about the way the company operates.

You may also try to find people who work at the company or are holding positions similar to ones that interest you, and ask them questions about their work and the company.

Further Resources and Literature:

Fry, Ron. *Your first interview*. The Career Press Inc.: Franklin Lakes, NJ, 2002, pp. 35-51
Gottesman, Deb, Mauro, Buzz. *The Interview Rehearsal Book,* Berkeley: New York, 1999
Kennedy, Joyce Lain. *Job Interviews for Dummies*. IDG Books Worldwide Inc.: Foster City, CA, 2000

Understand Job Requirements

The second step in preparing for a job interview is to understand the job requirements. Most job requirements are specified in classified want ads or in professional job listings found on company websites or on headhunter listings. Read each requirement carefully and be sure you understand the responsibilities that each requirement entails. For example, a job description for an electrical engineer could vary considerably from testing electrical components to designing printed circuit boards, to designing and building complex electronic systems. Be sure that you are comfortable with your ability to perform the particular requirements of a job before you go on the interview. Here again, if you can speak to someone within the company in a position similar to the one you are applying for, you can gleam helpful information first-hand about the job.

What to Bring to the Interview

Below is a checklist of items you need to bring to the interview. Consider assembling these items into an interview portfolio (see a detailed description of portfolio in Chapter 8, *Portfolio*).

Legal documents

Depending on your immigration status, you may need any of the following pieces of identification:

- Driver's license/identification card and/or passport/green card
- Personal identification card
- Social security card
- Travel documents.

Documents pertinent to your qualifications

- Additional copies of your resume
- Translated and notarized diplomas and transcripts
- Occupational licenses (if applicable). See the note on licenses in Chapter 2.

The following items can be added to your portfolio if applicable:

- Samples of your work. Here are some examples.
  o If you are a translator, samples of your translations
  o If you are an artist or a graphic designer, your portfolio
  o If you are an architect, photographs of the constructions you have designed
  o If you are an interpreter, newspaper clippings about the delegation in the area in which you acted as an interpreter (or any other evidence of your work)
- Professional publications including articles you authored
- Audio, videotapes or DVDs you are featured in. These can be used as evidence of your communication and public speaking skills
- Your certificates and awards relevant to the position you are seeking
- Photographs. These may include samples of your work.
- A notebook and a pen. A back up pen or pencil. **Do not rely on your memory; you will need to take notes.**

How to Dress and Groom

One of the first things recruiters notice about you is your dress and grooming. The impression you make speaks to your professionalism. Personal appearance is an important part of a professional image nearly everywhere in the world, including the United States. The general perception is that if you are well groomed and neatly dressed, you will take your job responsibilities seriously. If you are dressed properly, you are more likely to make a positive impression to your interviewer, including being viewed as organized, prepared, confident, and credible. Here are some suggestions for appropriate grooming and apparel for the job interview.

General Rule. Be neat and groomed — no multi-colored hair or excessive jewelry! Wear clothing that is clean, well cared-for, and (in most cases) conservative, i.e., clothing that is considered "business" attire by American standards. The following table provides general guidelines defining what is considered business attire for both men and women.

A quick reference table for acceptable American business attire

	Men	Women
Grooming	• Should be clean-shaven. • A neatly groomed mustache and beard are acceptable • Should not wear cologne	• Should shave their legs if any part of leg is visible • Should not wear perfume
Dress	• Solid color blue or gray suit (pin stripe is fine), white shirt, a conservative tie • Should avoid sleeveless tops unless wearing a jacket or sweater at all times. • No earrings or other jewelry (unless it is a college ring or wedding ring or you are interviewing for a designer job in a fashion magazine).	• Gray, black or blue suit, shoes with closed toe on a low or medium heel, neutral color pantyhose, minimal jewelry, no perfume, a conservative good-quality purse and/or good-quality leather brief case. It is fine to wear cosmetics to an interview, but use them sparingly and keep colors neutral. • Should avoid sleeveless tops unless wearing a jacket or sweater at all times

		• Absolutely NO "see through" blouse, deep cleavage or short midriff.

COMPARE

Make sure your personal hygiene is up to American standards. Unlike many other nationalities, Americans are very particular about body odors. They usually shower daily and use body deodorants and deodorant soaps.

Be sure that you shower before meeting with the interviewer; especially if you have a strong body odor and sweat excessively. Use antiperspirant deodorant to prevent sweating.

Do not use strong perfume. Many people in the US are allergic to perfume. You do not want to cause your employer to sneeze and feel uncomfortable!

Be aware that dress standards or business attire for employees will differ from industry to industry. For instance, the banking industry has a more formal dress code. In some industries, such as the entertainment or advertising industry, more casual clothing may be worn to work. In such industries, the dress code is considered "business casual," or "dress-down." Dress codes can also vary within a given company depending on the day of the week. In many companies, employees are permitted and even encouraged to dress in jeans[5] or khakis (chinos) on Fridays. This practice is called "casual Friday." If your interview is scheduled on Friday, find out if Friday is a casual day at the company. If it is, be less formal in your attire. Find out what "casual" really means to that organization. Ask the person who calls to make the interview appointment or others who work for the company. Does the company have a dress policy? It is better to dress in business attire vs. business casual – err on the side of caution and conservatism.

TIP FOR SUCCESS!

For your interview, it is always better to dress more formally than you would as an employee of the company. Dressing up shows your respect for the employer and a serious attitude towards the future job.

Business Casual Attire. Business casual is different from "weekend casual" and "casual Friday." For men this generally means a collared polo or golf shirt, loafer or oxford shoes, khakis, no tie. For women it means a dress, khakis, pants, skirts or cropped pants (below the knee, ankle length), blouse or sweater.

Every company has its own definition of business casual dress. However, be aware that if on a normal business day company employees do not wear ties, the recruiter will still expect a male candidate to wear a jacket and a tie to the interview and a female candidate to wear formal attire.

Preparing for Common Interview Questions

Although there is no limit to the variety of questions you may be asked during your interview, you can anticipate certain common questions and prepare your answers in advance. Typically, interviewers will ask you to describe your background and previous experience, your professional goals, how you performed in the past, and why you are interested to work for the company. This section contains a worksheet to help you prepare answers to these standard questions. By preparing and rehearsing your answers to these common questions, you will gain confidence in your ability to answer these and other questions that the interviewer may ask you on the spot.

---

[5] Jeans are not acceptable attire for most industries with an office environment, even on casual Fridays. They are acceptable most often in a warehouse or factory environment.

NOTE! *The kind of questions asked will depend on who is conducting the interview, i.e., the HR manager, department head, or your potential supervisor. Department managers will ask more specific, future job related technical questions.*

Many things go into a successful job interview that will lead to a job offer. Being able to answer the interviewer's questions and convince the employer that you are the best candidate for the job is a huge part of a successful job search.

Do you know what question you will be asked at the job interview almost 100% of the time? Read on.

After initial greeting and small talk (small talk means casual, not business related conversation), the interviewer will inevitably ask, "Tell me about yourself" or "Can you tell me about yourself?" This seems like a simple and easy question, right? This may in fact be the easiest question to answer; however, it is a very important one and you need to craft and practice your answer ahead of time. In Chapter 3, *Networking*, you learned how to put together your self-presentation to use when networking. Expand on it here and tailor it to the job for which you are applying. Here are some tips.

- One way to answer is to start with your education, and then list job experiences and any relevant personal information. For example, if your father and grandfather are engineers and you are applying for an engineering job, mention that you are a third generation engineer.

- You may also start by discussing your most recent relevant job experience and qualities you know are important to succeed in the American workplace. (See Chapter 1, *Qualities of an Ideal American Employee*).

Common Interview Questions Worksheet

So, what are you waiting for? Use the following worksheet to prepare your own answers to these most common interview questions. Write your answers in the spaces provided. Memorize and rehearse them, and you are on your way to success!

Selected Common Interview Questions

Q: *Tell me about yourself /your professional background.*
A: Here is a sample answer: *I am a teacher with five years experience in ... I am committed to my students' learning and have a lot of energy. I am constantly developing my knowledge of... and have taken additional responsibility for ...* Then you should talk about your relevant work experience, education, etc.

_____

_____

Q: *What do you consider some of your strong points?*

TIP FOR SUCCESS! *Check the job requirements specified by in the employment advertisement. Use examples from your professional/volunteer history to substantiate your answer. Chose three or four qualities (See in Chapter 1, Qualities of an Ideal American Employee), and elaborate on them using the examples from your professional history).*

_____

_____

Q: *What salary are you looking for?*

Specify a realistic salary range comparable to the going rate in the industry, your qualifications and geographic location. See more on salary issues in Chapter 7,

Chapter 4

TIP FOR SUCCESS!   *Negotiating an Offer.*

Note: You should anticipate this question and research the typical salary range in advance. Two good websites to get you started are salary.com and salaryexpert.com. Another way is to ask people who hold similar jobs. Remember, however, not to ask people what they make (asking people what they make is a rude question in the US). Instead ask if they know what the salary range is for a specific type of work. *Possible answer:* " *I expect to be paid a salary within the industry range.* "Then give a range. This discussion is usually deferred to the end of the interview.

Q: Why should we hire you?
Possible answer: List your personal characteristics such as being a hard worker, somebody who takes initiative to get the job done. Add your professional qualifications and relevant experience and accomplishments. Say: "I have _____(a degree) in _____field."

Q: Can you explain the gaps in your employment history?
Possible answer: To improve my education and training, I enrolled in the University.
Or here is another answer: "When we arrived in the US, took time off to improve my English language skills.

Q: Where do you see yourself in five years?

TIP FOR SUCCESS!
This answer should reflect your goals associated with the company. It is not a good idea to say, "I am planning to go into business for myself," or "I just view this as a temporary job before I find something better." A better answer would be "I see myself as a marketing director," if you are applying for a job in entry-level marketing. Or, "I envision myself as a team leader", if the position involves teamwork. Be prepared to elaborate.

Q: What is your weakest point?

TIP FOR SUCCESS!
Never answer that you do not have any weaknesses. *Experts in the field advise that the best way to handle this question is to admit to a minor weakness and then turn it into a positive quality (or as the Americans will say – "give it a positive spin"). Example: "Sometimes I have a problem delegating work; I stay late in the office or come in on weekends."*

Q: Why do you want to work for us?

Q: **Why did you apply for this position?**_____
_____
_____

Q: *What do you know about our company?*
_____
_____
_____

Q: *Tell me about your past jobs.*

TIP FOR SUCCESS! *Describe your past jobs emphasizing experience **relevant** to the position for which you are applying. Only discuss positive experiences. Even if you disliked your last job, think of something that you gained or learned from it and talk about that.*

Q: *Tell me about your education.*
_____
_____

Q: *What computer skills do you have?*

TIP FOR SUCCESS! *When describing your computer skills, add that you are constantly working on developing them. Mention courses you have taken and applications with which you are familiar.*

Q: *What are your most important accomplishments? What is the highest accomplishment you can name from your previous job?* (Use the samples from *Chapter 5, Promoting Your Accomplishments* as your guideline.)
_____
_____
_____
_____

Q: **Do you speak a foreign language?**

Suggested Answer: *Yes, my native language is _____ and I studied English in college and French in high school. I'd like to increase my fluency in French and I am constantly working on perfecting my English. To do that I took the following courses…*
_____
_____

Q: *Your resume does not list any job experience in the past year. Why?*

Possible answer: I took a year off to improve my English. It was a difficult decision but I knew that I needed to get my English skills up to par to be able to compete in the workplace.

During this past year I worked as a volunteer at…. I took evening ESL classes for advanced students and joined a local Toastmasters Club (see: Toastmasters in glossary) to develop my oral presentation skills. I believe it was the right decision and now I feel confident in my language skills and ready to devote myself to my career.

Q: *I see you grew up in India. Do you plan to go back there to live sometime in the future?*
Possible answer: "No. I prefer to live in this country. But on the other hand I would go wherever my career will take me." This is not an appropriate question to be asked in an interview but be prepared to answer it."

Q: *Why do you want to work in the US?*
Possible answer: This country has fascinated me since I was a child. To me the opportunity to work (with the leader in the industry) in the United States is exciting.

Q: What College did you attend?
Sample answer: "I went to _____ in St. Petersburg, Russia."

Q: *What was your major in college?*
Sample answer: I majored in (chemical engineering)_____ with a minor in_____(biology).

COMPARE *Some countries do not distinguish major and minor studies. You may briefly explain that and mention your areas of education.*

Q: *Do you get bored doing the same work over and over again?*
Suggested answer: Not really. I understand that work is not necessarily entertaining. Sometimes you just need to focus on what has to be done – even if it is not something new. I am always too busy to be bored. Be aware, however, that if the interviewer asks you this question, it is likely that the job may be repetitive and potentially uninteresting to you.

Q: *Do you prefer working alone or as a member of a team?*
Suggested answer: It depends on the best way to accomplish a project. Some projects are best done in a team environment and some need concentration on your own. I am capable of working within both environments.

Q: *What is your idea of success?*

Q: *Why have you had many jobs in short period of time?*

TIP FOR SUCCESS!
Explain the reason, then emphasize that now you want stability in your career.

NOTE!
If you are a recent college graduate, have been out of work for some time or are changing careers, you need to consider additional questions and answers. See the list of resources at the end of this chapter.

Illegal Interview Questions

What questions are illegal in the US? Inquiries related to the candidate's religion, race, place of birth, disability, marital status (especially if the person is a woman of childbearing age), age (candidates older than 40), or national origin are considered to be inappropriate and even illegal.

NOTE!
According to US law, all people should be treated equally. For this reason, employers are required to ask only non-discriminatory job related questions. Federal law forbids employers from discriminating against any person on the basis of race, national origin, religion, sex, or age. The final hiring decision should not be based on these factors or family connections.

Nevertheless, if you are asked, for example, what religion you practice, avoid showing anger or disapproval. Anticipating such illegal questions will help maintain composure. Keep in mind, however, that you may not want to work for an employer who would put you in this uncomfortable position. In any case, do not mention that the question is illegal.

CAUTION!
Do not react in angry fashion when you are asked an illegal or tactless question. Be as pleasant as possible. Anticipating the illegal question will help you to tone down your reaction.

To learn more about illegal interview questions and how to handle them, check out the following resources. Look for current up-to-date resources in your local library or book store.

Graber, Steven. *The everything get a job book.* Adams Media Corporation, Avon, USA, 2000, pp. 261-263

Chapter 4

Eyler, David R. *Job interviews that mean business*. New York, 1999, pp.175-180.

Preparing Your Own Questions

More often than not, at the conclusion of the interview you will be asked, "Do you have any questions?" You may have written down some questions that occurred to you during the course of the interview, but it is important to have a list of your own questions compiled ahead of time. There are four major areas that you should ask about: the industry, the company, the department, and the job for which you are applying.

TIP FOR SUCCESS! *Listen attentively. In the course of the interview, the interviewer may address some of the questions you have prepared. Make sure to check off questions that have been answered. It is better not to ask any questions at all than to ask the questions which were already covered in the course of the interview!*

If you ask a question about something that was already covered in an interview, the interviewer will assume that you did not listen or understand what he or she had said to you. This will score points against you as a candidate who does not have good listening skills. However, you may need to ask the interviewer to clarify information you didn't understand during the interview by restating the question. For example, *"In other words, you mean..."* or *"Would you repeat that please?"* or *"Did I get you right that...?"*

Start by asking easy general questions. Examples: *What is a typical workday like?* Then you can move to more job-specific questions, such as, *How would you describe an ideal candidate for this job?* or *What do you consider to be the three most important duties of the position?* Take notes on the answers — you will essentially get a script for your follow-up letter (see Chapter 5, *The Follow-up Letter*).

Sample Questions. In general, three to five questions are enough. You don't want to take too much of the interviewer's time. Here are some sample questions to ask.

- What are the three major responsibilities of the job, in order of priority?
- How do you see the department growing in the next few years?
- In your opinion, what is the worst (and the best) part of the job?
- If I am hired, to whom will I report?
- What is the typical career path for the position?
- Which clients will be assigned to me?
- Is travel expected?
- How many others are interviewing for this position?
- What kind of training programs do you provide?
- Why did the last person leave this job?
- How does your company measure employee performance?
- How would you describe the management philosophy of this company?
- When do you think you will be making a hiring decision?
- What is the next step?

The questions listed above are of a general nature. You will need to think of more specific questions as well. For instance, if during the interview for an engineering job your interviewer mentions a specific piece of equipment, you might ask a question regarding the equipment design.

When asking a specific question, make sure to use industry terms, or lingo. Prepare notes in advance. Ask the interviewer if it is OK to refer to them.

WARNING!

Until you get a formal job offer, do not bring up questions about salary, vacations and other benefit issues.

Handling Immigration Status Questions

Title VII of the Civil Rights Act of 1964 provides protection on the basis of national origin. A prominent career expert, David Eyler in his book *Interviews That Mean Business* advises to be honest about your immigration status, but not "to make an issue of it." If asked at the interview, state the category of visa that you hold and, if possible, leave the details of what that means until you have an offer. In the US, discrimination on the basis of your "foreignness" or the fact that you have an accent or non-white skin color is illegal. However, at the early stages of the job selection process these factors could contribute to the decision to screen you out.

If you need the company's help to sponsor your work visa, do not bring up the issue during the initial or screening interview (unless asked). Keep in mind that some employers may be unwilling to sponsor you because of the cost and paperwork involved and possible complications.

If you need the employer's sponsorship, mention it during the interview or after you have received a job offer. If you tell the employer what steps to take to arrange your visa, you might be able to eliminate or diminish any reluctance to sponsor you.

Any employer serious about hiring you will retain an immigration attorney to arrange your work visa. Some companies provide visa support to their international employees as a part of their benefits package.

In either case, you need to understand your immigration status and visa options open to you and your family. (See the list of resources in Chapter 1, *Who Can Work in the US?*)

Diversity in the Workplace and You

What is diversity? In this book diversity is defined as variety of races and national cultures (with their languages, values, customs and traditions). In general diversity goes much further.

Although among some Americans 9/11 events led to some mistrust of foreigners, in recent years, especially after tragic 9/11 events, there is a strong movement toward embracing and managing diversity in this country. The general concept of diversity in the US includes age, race, gender, sexual orientation, religion, disabilities, and ethnicity. On the whole, American companies and most Americans embrace diversity. You may see a bumper sticker or a T-shirt reading *Unity in Diversity*. More and more employees are being trained on how to develop good working relationships with people from cultures other than their own.

You can encounter two kinds of recruiters: those who understand and embrace diversity, and those who do not and have only superficial knowledge of it. However, companies are realizing the costs associated with ignoring diverse population groups. The main costs are lawsuits, loss of business to certain customer groups, decrease of productivity as a result of misunderstanding, and weakened morale among employees.

TIP FOR SUCCESS!

A good approach during the interview is to emphasize your bilingual or multilingual skills, networking in ethnic communities, travel experience, and understanding of different cultures. Think of the examples that show how your non-American background can be beneficial for the business.

Chapter 4

"I hear, and I forget. I see, and I remember. I do, and I understand."
A Chinese proverb.

Practicing an Interview

Some people (and they are very few) can acquire skills by just reading. Most people acquire a skill or competence by practicing it. To be at your best during the interview, you need to practice it. Have a friend (preferably an American) help you to prepare by acting as an interviewer. Have him or her ask questions and critique your responses. In other words, conduct a mock (not real) interview.

Use video technology to tape yourself in a mock interview. Watch the video. Have a friend critique your performance. Using this technique guarantees an improved performance. See *Interview Evaluation Score Card* following this section.

Demeanor, speaking, listening and contents are the four major dimensions you should be aware of when preparing for the interview. Try to incorporate the following qualities in your interview.

Demeanor
- ❑ Be friendly, relaxed, and confident.
- ❑ Maintain eye contact, but do not stare. If there is more than one interviewer, be sure to make eye contact with each of them throughout the interview.

TIP FOR SUCCESS!
A meeting of the eyes between two people that occurs when they look directly at each other is called "eye contact" in the US.

COMPARISON
Compare: in some countries it is disrespectful to maintain eye contact, especially with people of higher status or the opposite sex. In the U.S., it is considered good manners to make eye contact with the person with whom you are conversing. In other countries, eye contact is too intense for American standards.

Speaking
- ❑ Speak clearly, enunciate.
- ❑ Watch your grammar and vocabulary. Develop a list of your industry-specific vocabulary, terms, acronyms, expressions.
- ❑ Use industry terms whenever appropriate.

Listening
- ❑ Lean forward slightly and nod while the other party is speaking.
- ❑ Do not interrupt!
- ❑ Smile sincerely.

Contents
- ❑ Be positive. Highlight your qualifications, successes, achievements, and abilities.
- ❑ Downplay your weaknesses. Don't bring them up unless asked. When asked, put a positive spin on your answer.
- ❑ When answering questions, tailor them to the job requirements and what American employers are looking for in their employees.

NOTE!
Positive *means optimistic, constructive, encouraging, believing in "happy" endings. Being positive is very important American value.*

Here are some tips on practicing for an interview.

Tips on How to Practice for an Interview
1. *Read the questions (see: Common Interview Questions in this chapter).*
2. *Customize questions where necessary.*
3. *Compile answers customizing the suggestions provided in the worksheet.*

4. *Practice in front of a mirror.*
5. *Tape the questions and your answers.*
6. *Play the cassette whenever you have free time. The best time to rehearse in general is the evening and morning. If you rehearse right before you go to bed and then repeat first thing in the morning, you will memorize your lines better.*
7. *Practice your answers over and over again and watch your confidence grow!*

Interview Practice Score Card

Practice your interview with the help of this scorecard. Have your friend act as a recruiter. Conduct your first interview using the scorecard. Work on one skill at a time. Be patient — it will take several tries to see an improvement.

Exercise

This exercise will help you identify the areas in which you need to improve. Make several copies of the scorecard. Practice the interview several times recording your progress. Watch yourself improve!
Watch yourself on the VCR or DVD, and, rate yourself or have a friend rate and evaluate your tape. Rate from one to three. One is the lowest; three is the highest.

INTERVIEW PRACTICE			
BEHAVIOR			
Score	1	2	3
Appearance			
Handshake			
Confidence			
Eye contact			
Smile			
Posture			
INTERVIEW START			
Score	1	2	3
Small Talk			
INTERVIEW			
Handling Questions			
Using Examples			
Emphasizing Positive			
Downplaying negative			
Asking own questions			
CONCLUSION			
Score	1	2	3
Thanking interviewer for her or his time Asking when the decision will be made			
Saying goodbye			
LANGUAGE			
Score	1	2	3
Clarity/ Enunciation (Specify what was not clear, grammar)			

List three grammar mistakes			
List three pronunciation mistakes			
Words and expressions used			
Recommendations on grammar			
Recommendations on pronunciation			
Strengths (specify) 1. 2. 3.			
Areas for Improvement (Specify) 1. 2. 3.			

Interview Types

Your preparation and skill development practiced in the previous section will prepare you for any job interview, regardless of the mode or form of the interview. It is helpful to know that interviews vary by

- mode of conducting (in person or telephone, video, on-line interview)
- interviewing structure (one-on-one vs. group interview)
- interviewing approach (traditional, behavioral, case question interview)
- interview site (on-site or over a meal or coffee in a restaurant).

In most cases, you will be interviewed in person, one-on-one, in the office. Regardless of the interview type and venue, there are basic guidelines for a successful job interview. Having appropriate qualifications for the job and following these guidelines will better enable you to secure the job offer. Now, let's examine different types of interviews.

Face-to-Face (In-Person) Interviews

In this type of interview, the applicant and potential employer meet in person. Normally, the meeting is held at the employer's office. This is the most common type of interview.

Phone Interview

The applicant is interviewed over the phone. Generally, the purpose of this type of interview is to screen out inappropriate candidates. If the applicant passes the phone interview, he or she will be invited for an interview in person. Generally speaking, it is challenging to make a positive impression over the phone and to make your phone interview successful. It is especially challenging if English is not your first language. However, one benefit is that you can refer to notes or other reference materials without worrying about making eye contact or the appearance of reading from a script. Below are some tips to help you with the phone interview process.

- Take the call in an isolated room, so there are no interruptions and you can concentrate fully on the conversation.
- Have a copy of your resume handy so that you can refer to it during the conversation.

- Prepare a list of questions to ask the interviewer. Refer to *Preparing your own questions* earlier in this chapter.
- Another useful question to ask is *"What is your biggest challenge?"* Find out the employer's needs or problems and sell yourself as a person who is able to fill those needs or solve those problems.
- Sound enthusiastic, energetic, and positive.
- Smile. It may feel funny to smile into the telephone, but if you smile, your personality will come across as friendly and cheerful. You may consider placing a mirror in front of you so that you could watch your facial expression and see if you are smiling.

TIP FOR SUCCESS!

Keep a mirror at your desk. Glance into it while you are on the phone to remind yourself to smile.

- Project your voice, speak clearly, and enunciate. If you stand up, it is easier to do this. If you are sitting down, relax and lean back in your chair. You will sound more relaxed and confident.
- Try to limit your responses to three-to-four short sentences. Stay on target — don't ramble (speak to the point).

Computerized Interview

Computerized interviewing utilizes a computer to ask the questions. Similar to the phone interview, this technique is also used primarily for screening purposes. The candidate comes in and answers the questions or performs tasks electronically. This kind of interview may also be conducted on-line.

Video-conferencing Interview

Thanks to new technology, the job applicant and the employer can sometimes get together on-line. Interviews can now be conducted over the Web; it just requires access to a computer, the Internet, and a video monitor. You and the interviewer will hear and see each other and interact directly. On the whole, the preparation is the same as any other interview. However, you should be aware of possible lag time, delay between verbal communication (sound) and the moving image. For example, you may hear the phrase and then see the other person's lips moving afterwards.

The Group Interview

You may be interviewed by more than one person at a time. Be sure to smile, maintain eye contact, and interact with as many people as you can. Get the names and business cards of all those present. You will need this contact information to mail the follow-up letters.

Behavioral Interview

What is behavioral interviewing? Behavioral interviewing is based on the premise that a person's recent, relevant past performance is the best predictor of future performance. Instead of asking how you *would* behave in a particular situation, a behavioral interviewer will ask how you *did* behave. You will be asked to provide a specific example of a past situation or task to demonstrate the way you performed in that specific situation or task.

How should you answer a behavioral question? First of all, prepare for an interview by recalling recent situations that show favorable behaviors or actions involving job requirements. Be sure that each story has a beginning (introduction), middle (body), and end (conclusion). Be specific. Don't generalize about several events; give a detailed account of one event. Use the STAR technique described below to structure your answer. Expect the interviewer to question and probe; for example, *"What did you say?" "What did you do?" " What was your role?"*

The goal of the behavioral interview is to predict future behavior by examining past behavior. While traditional interviews rely on general questions, behavioral written assessment tools and/or interviews utilize behavior-based specific questions. You will be expected to answer those questions using an example from your personal experience. Each example should be worded in what we refer to as STAR format.

"How do you handle criticism from other people" (traditional-style question) vs. "Tell me about a time when your work was criticized" (behavior-based question). This particular question is aimed at learning about the candidate's leadership skills.

COMPARISON

Many recruiters expect you to use STAR format when conducting behavioral interview. Here is the template complete with an example.

S Situation or Task: Briefly outline a situation or task you have encountered that will make a point about one of your skills or strengths.

T *Example: Training department did not have roles and responsibilities defined. As a result team members were inefficient in their work. Needed to insure that every team member knows their responsibilities.*

A Action: Describe the specific actions you took to meet your objective.

Example: Created a spreadsheet identifying roles and responsibilities, held a team meeting. Explained member roles and responsibilities.

R Result: Summarize the positive results of your action. If the results are quantifiable provide dollar amount, numbers or percentage.

Example: Team members now know what their roles and responsibilities are. This knowledge dramatically improved (tripled) operations efficiency.

A good way to prepare for a behavioral interview is to
- Go through your resume line by line and recollect relevant examples;
- Write out and edit the answer;
- Rehearse your answer.

Exercise: Behavioral Interview Questions
Now complete the following exercise to find out how good you are at answering behavioral interview questions. *Tip: Use your resume and describe examples substantiating what is in your resume.* Using the STAR format fill out the right column of the exercise below.

Leadership

Question	Possible Answer
Use **STAR** format: **S**ituation, **T**ask, **A**ction, **R**esults	
Describe how you set an example for other employees.	

Teamwork

Question	Possible Answer
Tell me about a time when you worked with others to complete a project or to achieve a goal. What was the situation? What was your role specifically? What did you contribute to the team results? What was the end result? How did you feel about working with people on the team? What was the outcome?	

Breakfast/Lunch/Dinner Interview. Sometimes an interview may happen over a meal. It can be any of the three meals, breakfast, lunch, or dinner. The lunch interview is the most common. In order to be successful in this kind of interview, you need to know American table etiquette. (See Chapter 8, *American Table Etiquette,* for details on how to conduct yourself during a meal interview.)

Networking (Informational, Exploratory) Interview. An informational (exploratory, networking) interview is normally requested by the job seeker with the intention of learning about the company or the position. An informational interview can be a meeting with a potential employer. You can also have an informational interview with a person who is employed at the company and has a position similar to the one you are seeking. Although it is possible to get a job offer as a result of an informational interview, that is not its purpose. The goal is to get to know the person who makes the hiring decision and to get information on the company, job openings, etc. Remember, *you are the person who is asking questions,* not the other party. When crafting your questions, have in mind three goals:

- to get information
- to tell about yourself (make it known that you are available for hire)
- to build relationships

The following are sample questions that can be asked at an informational interview:

- How did you get where you are today?
- Among the leaders in your field, who might be looking for someone with my skills?
- What are your biggest challenges?
- Could you name organizations that might need employees with my background?

More sample questions in given in Chapter 3.

You will need an introductory sentence when requesting or starting an informational interview, such as, I'd like to broaden my knowledge of the company and find out how a person with my experience level can gain appropriate employment.

NOTE! *As with the job interview, always write a thank you letter after your networking interview.*

Sample Networking Interview Thank You Letter

Date Name Company Address *Dear ...:* *Thank you for taking the time to meet with me on Wednesday. I enjoyed speaking with you and learning about the diversity programs at All-American Company.* *Our discussion definitely strengthened my interest in Human Resources as a career path. I am planning to take your advice and subscribe to HR Magazine. I will also get in touch with the contacts that you provided to inquire about job possibilities.* *Sincerely,* Szilvia Gwazda

Chapter 4

Case interview. Case question interviews test you on your ability to solve problematic situations. Sometimes the companies expect you to write out your answer, other times to talk about your solution to a problematic situation. Find out more about case interview in Marc P. Cosentono's book *Case in Point: Complete Case Interview Preparation* or in *The Vault Guide to the Case Interview*.

Further Resources and Literature:

David R. Eiler. *Job Interviews That Mean Business,* p. 17-19
Adams, Bob. *The everything job interview book.* Bob Adams Media Corporation, Avon, Massachusetts, Random House, New York, 2001, p.175-195 (discusses legal issues in detail).
Fry, Ron. *101 Great Answers To the Toughest Interview Questions*. Forth Edition. Career Press, Franklin Lakes, NJ.
Ingols, Cynthia and Shapiro, Mary. *Your job interview.* Barnes & Noble Basics. Silver Lining Books, 2003.
Moreira, Paula. *Ace the IT interview!* Osborne/MsGraw Hill, New York, 2002 *Great answers to over 200 tough interview questions*. Bob Adams media corporation, Avon, Massachusetts, 2004
Power interviews. Job winning tactics from Fortune 500 Recruiter. John Wiley and Sons, Inc. New York, 1998.
Yates, Martin. *Great answers to over 200 tough interview questions*. Bob Adams media corporation, Avon, Massachusetts, 2004.

Moving On

Now that you have learned how to prepare for an interview, Step 3 in the Job Search process), and know about different interview formats, it's time to move on to Chapter 5 – *Conducting the Interview*.

Chapter Glossary

Annual report: a document containing financial information sent out to shareholders of publicly traded companies on yearly basis. Information pertains to company profits, revenue, and expenses.
Award: prize or reward for accomplishments
Bring up: mention, speak of
Bumper sticker: a sticker with an image or words on a car bumper
Casual attire: informal clothing
Casual day: a day of the week, normally Friday, when employees are expected to dress casually
CEO (abbreviation): Chief Executive Officer
Check off: consider done
Company culture: the way things are done in the company
Credible: (professionally) trustworthy
Delegate (a job or task): entrust, hand over
Demeanor: manner, conduct, behavior
Disability: physical limitation of some kind
Discrimination: bias, unfairness, prejudice
Downplay: tone down, make it sound less significant
Dress up: dress more formally
Dress down: dress less formally

Embrace: accept
Employee handbook: a booklet created and distributed by a company (generally for its own employees) outlining its rules, procedures, and code of conduct.
Enunciate: speak clearly and distinctly
Eye contact: a meeting of the eyes between two people that occurs when they look directly at each other
Face-to-face (in-person) interview: when an applicant and a potential employer meet in person.
Golf shirt: a shirt with collar
Hire: to employ
Highlight: emphasize
Illegal: against the law, unlawful
Initial Interview: first interview
Lingo: industry-specific language, terms, buzz words
On paper: an American idiom for what something appears to be in writing (the ideal); it is used to contrast with what that something is in reality

Off-site: outside company's facilities
Perfectionist: very thorough person (more than is necessary)
Phone interview: when an applicant is interviewed over the phone
Pin stripe: fabric with very thin (pin width) stripes
Polo (shirt): a casual shirt without collar
Positive: optimistic, constructive, encouraging, believing in "happy" end
Project (one's voice): speak loudly and clearly, speak with strong voice
Review (performance review): evaluation of employee performance
Score points: make a favorable impression
Screening interview: first interview conducted with the purpose to exclude inappropriate candidates
Sponsor: support (e.g., work visa), fund, subsidize
STAR: (**s**ituation **t**ask **a**ction **r**esult) interviewing technique based on the premise that a person's recent, relevant past performance is the best predictor of future performance.
Tone down: to moderate, to make less pronounced, softer
T-shirt: a casual shirt without sleeves
VCR or DVD: a device that replays a recorded moving image onto a screen
Web-cam: a small device attached to a computer enabling transmission of moving image
9/11 (events): September 11, 2001 bombing of World Trade Center in New York City. This date is date of mourning in the US.

Chapter 5

Step 4: *PROMOTE YOURSELF CONFIDENTLY AT THE INTERVIEW*

In this Chapter: ● Your arrival ● Making a great first impression ● Interview stages – Promoting your accomplishments ● Concluding the interview ● Chapter summary ● Moving on

At last you are invited to the long-anticipated job interview, the opportunity to promote yourself to the employer face-to-face using the skills and knowledge acquired in Chapter 4. In this chapter we will focus on the specific behavior, protocol, and rules of etiquette you should follow during the interview to make the best possible impression on your interviewer(s). The interview process begins with your arrival. Let's get started.

Your Arrival

Your arrival at the employer's office or interview site is the first important step towards a successful interview. **Never be late for the interview**. Always plan to arrive 10-15 minutes prior to your scheduled appointment time.

COMPARISON

In some countries, tardiness is tolerated. However, in the US, arriving late creates a negative impression. Americans often have tight schedules and therefore place high value on time. If you are late for your interview, you will jeopardize your success at the very start. Remember the very American saying, "Time is money".

Yes, be on time, but also be prepared to wait! While this may seem rude on the part of the employer, some interviewers will make you wait just to test how you react when things do not go according to plan or schedule. If you must wait, be patient and stay composed. Use the time to your advantage by reviewing your notes, reading company brochures, observing the surroundings, and making note of company awards and slogans. You can often use the information gathered during your wait to impress the interviewer with your knowledge of the company.

Making a Great First Impression

In Chapter 4, you prepared for your interview and rehearsed the meeting. Now is the time to act! While interfacing with people in the company, realize that you have only one chance to make a great first impression. The first several minutes of a meeting are critical to creating a favorable first impression. I heard one recruiter say, "I know in the first five minutes if I like the candidate or not!"

Let's go through the sequence of events that occurs during a typical interview greeting and point out the specific behaviors that will help you to make a great first impression:

- Your evaluation is likely to begin with the first person you meet when you enter the room, typically a receptionist, secretary, or administrative assistant. Smile warmly. Americans like to deal with friendly people. Smiling in the US is not only a standard greeting; it is a sign of friendliness. Identify yourself to the receptionist stating that you are here for an interview. For example, you might say, "*Hello, I am (Your Name). I am here for an interview with (Interviewer's Name).*" The receptionist usually asks you to take a seat while the interviewer is notified of your arrival. (If you are asked to wait for a period of time, you can use this time to review your notes or gather additional company information.)

Usually the first person the candidate meets is a receptionist/secretary/office attendant. Treat her or him as an extension of the interviewer. In the US, sometimes making a good impression with that first person counts for a lot. When the interviewer arrives and the attendant smiles, the interviewer knows that the candidate has already made a good impression with the lower-level staff member and therefore likely treats employees of all job levels with respect.

NOTE!

- If you are sitting down when the interviewer arrives, make sure you stand up to greet him/her.

- Let the interviewer speak first, then say: *"Hello, I am (Your Name). I am pleased to meet you, (Interviewer's Name)."* Use the formal Mr., Mrs., Ms., or Dr., as applicable, when addressing the interviewer until you are invited to use his or her first name. Always use Ms. (pronounced "miz") to address a woman recruiter, unless she indicates that she prefers "Miss" or "Mrs." [Note: In the US workplace, it is common for the subordinate to address a supervisor by his or her first (given) name.]

- Maintain eye contact.

- Be relaxed, **confident** and attentive. (I emphasize "confidence" because Americans put high value on confidence in their employees.)

- Wait until the recruiter extends his or her hand for a handshake. When shaking hands, make sure to offer a firm grip. The handshake should last two seconds. Americans associate a weak handshake with a weak personality. Remember that confidence is valued highly in American workplace.

If your handshake is weak, Americans will assume that you are lacking in confidence. Keep in mind that if the handshake is too long (more than a couple of seconds) or too firm (to the point that it may hurt), Americans become uncomfortable.

NOTE!

In some countries, such as Russia, it is rude to extend your hand for a handshake to a woman unless she extends her hand first. A man has to wait until a woman extends her hand first. Not in the US!

COMPARISON

- Before you sit down, wait for the interviewer either to sit down first or indicate that you should be seated.

- At all times, keep your posture straight and smile warmly.

To help you remember the important points in making a great first impression, recall the **SHE™** formula:

SHE™	**S = Smile** Smile warmly when you arrive. Americans like to deal with friendly people. Smiling in the US is not only a standard greeting; it is a sign of friendliness.
	H = Handshake If your handshake is weak, Americans will assume that you are lacking in confidence. <u>Americans put high value on confidence in their employees</u>. If the handshake is too long (more than a couple of seconds) or too firm (to the point that it may hurt), Americans become *uncomfortable*.
	E = Eye Contact Maintain eye contact. This means looking the interviewer in the eye.

Use the SHE™ formula to always remember to smile, shake hands, and make eye contact with your interviewer.

Interview Stages

Following the initial greetings between interviewers and candidate, the interview itself typically proceeds in four stages:

Stage 1: The interviewer will begin with small talk (polite informal conversation).

Stage 2: The interviewer will tell you about the company and briefly describe the position.

Stage 3: The interviewer will ask you questions pertaining to the position.

Stage 4: You will be given the opportunity to ask your own questions.

Anticipating these stages will help you to be confident while conducting the interview. Let's look at each stage more closely.

Stage 1: Small Talk

Small talk is simply a transition to the stages of dialogue that will follow. The interviewer may lead with a few informal questions such as:

Questions	*Suggested Replies*
What is the weather like out there?	*The weather is great. I like this time of year.*
It is beautiful outside, isn't it?	*Yes, it is.*
How was your ride in?	*Great. Thank you.*
Did you have any problem finding us?	*No, not at all. I studied the directions.*

During the small talk stage, keep your answers cheerful, short and crisp (no more than one or two short sentences), as shown in the examples above.

CAUTION!

Do not go into lengthy descriptions of how tiresome the ride was, or how you missed the exit on the highway, etc.

Following small talk, the interview moves to Stage 2, description of the position.

Stage 2: Description of the Position

The interviewer will briefly describe the position. You should:

Listen carefully

Take notes (but not dictation) to capture the main points of the interview. First, ask the interviewer for permission to take notes: "Do you mind if I take notes?" Your notes will help you to write a follow-up letter after the interview.

Interject tactfully. As the employer describes the duties that your job will entail, listen carefully. Draw parallels between the company's needs and your own experiences. Interject tactfully and demonstrate your familiarity with the subject. For instance, say "Oh, yes, I have done this type of work in my previous position."

After the position description dialogue, the interview will move to the third stage, answering the questions posed by the interviewer.

Stage 3: Answering Questions

In this stage, the interviewer will ask you questions to determine your suitability for the job. You will be well prepared for this stage if you have read and completed the exercises in Chapter 4.

COMPARE

Even if you are a modest person by nature, or your culture does not encourage self-promotion, remember that during the interview you are expected to talk about your positive traits and your accomplishments.

Follow these important tips during the question and answer (Q&A) phase of the interview.

Be sure to **maintain eye contact**, be attentive, and give brief but complete answers to questions. (Look the interview in the eyes but do not stare.)

Smile naturally when you speak.

Always project an air of **confidence and conviction** when answering a question. Maintaining eye contact and smiling will help you do this.

Whenever possible, **cite an example or evidence of your experience** that supports your answer. (See how to best present your accomplishments in the discussion *Promote your accomplishments,* which follows these tips) .

If you are not sure that you understood the question, **ask for clarification**.

- You can say, *"Would you please repeat that?"* or *"Would you mind repeating your question?"* You can also say, *"Excuse me?"*, although this phrase is more appropriate in less formal situations, such as at parties.

- Another way to check your understanding is to paraphrase (restate) a question or statement back to the interviewer. For instance, *"In other words, you would like to know if..."*

Do not apologize for your poor English.

TIP FOR SUCCESS!

If you have a good sense of humor, make fun of your accent. If the interviewer did not understand you, just smile and say, "It is my accent" and repeat the phrase again.

Emphasize the positive; downplay the negative. I cannot emphasize enough the importance of being positive. Americans feel very uncomfortable around negative people. Even if you are asked about the worst job experience you have had, be sure to highlight what you have learned from that experience. In other words, show your optimism. Present all of your experiences, even the bad ones, as learning experiences.

Never speak negatively about your current or past job, boss or co-worker, or your country of origin.

Utilize your portfolio. It is an effective way to demonstrate your qualifications and achievements (See *Chapter 8, Portfolio*).

Promoting Your Accomplishments

"It does not matter how good you are if nobody knows about you."
- Unknown

If you do not tell the interviewers about your achievements, they will assume that you do not have any. Be sure to provide examples to substantiate the answers to the interviewer's questions. The two scenarios below illustrate how you can promote your accomplishments.

TIP FOR SUCCESS!

Do not be too wordy or exaggerate. Instead, in several sentences describe the steps you took to accomplish a goal or task.

Example 1:

Job requirements: *team builder, leadership skills.*

Accomplishments should be listed as bullet points on your resume, such as: *Developed new hire training program by building teams of subject matter experts in various areas of business.* Use the "BPS formula" (Background, Problem, and Solution). Discuss your accomplishments in the following way:

1. **Background.** Start with setting the stage: *"I was once hired to develop a new hire program."*

2. **Problem** . Then describe the situation: *"I encountered unstructured training in which new hires merely watched other experienced employees perform their daily tasks. This kind of training was quite inefficient."*

3. **Solution**. Describe the solution: *"Through my implementation of regular meetings, documenting business knowledge by taping training sessions, assembling a list of industry and company terms, and creating structured presentations, exercises and other activities, the team was able to convert chaotic training into a structured program, complete with presentations, exercises and tests."*

Example 2:

Job requirement: *Goal-oriented*

Accomplishment: *Developed excellent presentation skills*

1. **Background.** *Three years ago I was a new employee at Customer Service, Inc., where oral communication skills were very important. The position was especially challenging for me because English is not my native language.*

2. **Problem.** *I realized that in order to advance in my job I needed to develop my communication skills.*

3. **Solution.** *I joined a community Toastmasters Club. On joining the club, I scheduled ten speeches from the basic communication manual. By the fifth speech I felt that I had greatly improved. By my tenth speech, I had improved so much that I received a promotion; the requirement for my new position was excellent communication skills! Meanwhile, I was invited to speak at the local Rotary Club and at the Chamber of Commerce. Now I consider my presentation skills to be my strength.*

After the interviewer finishes asking you questions, he/she will give you the opportunity to ask questions of your own in the next stage of the interview.

Stage 4: Asking Questions

When the interviewer invites you to ask questions, ask three to five questions. Refer to the list of suggested questions in *Chapter 4, Preparing Your Own Questions.*

WARNING!

Until you get a formal job offer, do not bring up questions about salary, vacations and other benefit issues.

Be respectful but do not be shy. If you find that you want the position, ask for it. As a rule, directness is appreciated in America. For example, *"At this time, do you foresee anything that would prevent you from offering me the position?"* If this brings out any objections, you will have the opportunity to address them right on the spot or in your follow-up letter.

After the interviewer has answered your questions about the job and the company, the interview usually comes to a conclusion.

Concluding the Interview

At the end of the interview, typically the interviewer will stand up, thank you, and extend his or her hand. You should shake the hand firmly and thank the interviewer. If you did not get the interviewer's business card earlier, make sure to ask for it now. You will need to know the exact spelling of the interviewer's name, phone number and address to follow up with a letter and/or phone calls. Finally, be sure to ask the interviewer, *"What is the next step in the hiring process?"*

TIP FOR SUCCESS!

At the conclusion of the interview, make sure that you remember to ask for the interviewer's business card. You will need the information on the card to write the follow- up letter.

Chapter Summary

Let's summarize the most important points to remember in order to make a great first impression and to ensure a successful job interview:

- Arrive on time.
- Greet everyone, including office assistants, with a friendly smile.
- Be patient and resourceful if you have to wait to meet the interviewer.
- Stand up when greeting the interviewer.

- Smile and maintain eye contact
- Know the four stages of the interview (small talk, description of the position, answering questions, asking questions)
- When telling about your accomplishments, use the 3S formula (setting, situation, solution)
- At the conclusion: 1) thank the interviewer, 2) remember to ask for the business cards, and 3) ask what is the next step in the hiring process.

Moving On

Congratulations! You've made it though the most challenging part of the job search process, the interview. You feel good about your performance and confident about your chances of getting the job. You may wish to relax a bit; perhaps you ask yourself, *"Do I wait for the recruiter to call me for a second interview or possibly offer me the job?"* The answer is **no**! There is one more important step to do. After your interview, you need to be **proactive,** which means taking certain actions to increase your chances of getting the job offer. We will discuss these actions in Chapter 6, *Increase Your Chances by Following Up,* which is Step 5 in the *How to Get a Job* process.

Useful Resources and Literature:

Eiler, David R. *Job interviews that mean business*. Random House, NY, 1999
Allen, Jeffrey. J.D., C.P.C. *The complete Q&A Job Interview Book.* John Wiley and Sons. New York, 1988.
Ingols, Cynthia and Shapiro, Mary. *Your job interview.* Barnes & Noble books, New York, 2003.

Chapter Glossary

Customer service: servicing customers, helping customers
Credentials: qualifications (including diplomas, etc.)
Culture: traditions, customs, way of doing things
Downplay: underemphasize
Follow up: take additional action to ensure that an earlier endeavor is successful
Goal oriented: focused on goals
On the spot: immediately

Portfolio: samples of work
Proactive: taking action; not waiting for something or someone else to take action
Problem solving: ability to solve business problems
Project (an air of confidence): appear to be confident
Small talk: non-business related, social conversation

Chapter 6

Step 5: Increase Your Chances by Following Up

In this Chapter: ● Follow-up (thank-you) letter ● Follow-up phone calls ● Chapter Summary ● Moving On ● Review of Chapters 1 through 6

> *"Getting hired is still not over. Getting hired is still up to you."*
> *Jeffrey Allen, a leading employment attorney*

Since you most likely will be competing for the job with other excellent candidates, a good performance during the job interview may not guarantee a job offer. From the employer's perspective, and yours, the hiring process does not end with the departing handshake at the conclusion of the interview. Employers usually require some time to evaluate the finalists for the job before reaching a final decision on who to hire. For candidates who have been granted an interview, it is customary in the US to follow up the interview by sending a thank-you letter to the interviewer.

In this chapter, we will discuss Step 5 of the job search process – how to write a thank you letter and how to follow up with a phone call. Following up the interview is a short step compared to earlier steps but it is just as important as the earlier ones. As we shall see, your thank-you letter is more than a simple courtesy; it is a final chance to market yourself — it is an essential component of the self-marketing campaign. Follow-up is very important for two reasons. First, employers appreciate candidates who follow up effectively. Therefore it is to your advantage to be proactive and "strike while the iron is hot". Secondly, job-hunting in the US is competitive; if you don't follow up, your competitors who do will have an advantage over you.

The last impression you make can be just as important as the first. The thank-you letter and follow-up phone call are your opportunities to remind the employer of your visit and reinforce your qualifications and desire for the job. Performing these steps will dramatically improve your chances of being hired. Let's look at each of these, first the letter and then the phone call.

Follow-up (Thank-You) Letter

Always send a thank-you letter within 24 hours after every employment interview. It is your last chance to make a good impression.

COMPARE

In some countries the post-interview thank you letters are not usually part of the employment process. In others, along with simple expression of thanks, you may perhaps mention other qualifications that did not come up during the interview. In the US, unlike many other countries, the thank you letter is not so much an expression of thanks but another component of the self-marketing campaign.

In the US the follow-up letter is another opportunity to restate your interest in the company and your desire to be hired. In addition, you may include additional information about yourself that you did not have a chance to present during your interview.

TIP FOR SUCCESS! *Remember to write to each person you spoke to during the interview. Do not send an identical letter to each person on your list; rather personalize your letters by making each one a little different from the others.*

In your letter 1) thank the interviewer for his or her time, 2) express your continued interest in the position and your suitability for the job, 3) mention anything important that you either left out during the interview or wished you handled better in your answers.

You can handwrite the letter on good stationery or a thank-you card (if your handwriting is legible); or you can send a typed letter. If you know your interviewer's e-mail address, you can certainly send a thank you letter via e-mail. But keep in mind that a neatly typed or handwritten letter has a more formal quality and therefore can be a plus in your favor.

Here are a couple of sample letters you might consider:

Sample follow up letter #1

Your name
Street Address, phone, e-mail address

Date

Interviewer's name
Title
Company name
Street address
City, State, zip code

Dear Ms. (Mr., Mrs.):

[1] Thank the interviewer for her or his time. Mention some specifics about the interview to remind the interviewer who you are.
I am writing to thank you for interviewing me on... (date, e. g., Sept 28) for the chemical engineer position. It was especially informative to meet you at your Tampa plant. I was very impressed with the _____ equipment (identify specific equipment by name) you had at this location.

[2] Restate your interest in the company and the position, and mention why you are a good candidate for the job. In addition, you can add another piece of information about yourself that you did not have the chance to present during your interview.
I would like to reiterate that I am very interested in the position. I believe I have the combination of education and experience to do the job.

[3] Suggest providing additional information at the interviewer's request. You may also mention that you will follow up with a phone call in a few days.
If I can provide you with additional information, please let me know. I look forward to hearing from you soon.

Sincerely,

Raj Kapoor

Raj Kapoor

Here is another follow-up/thank-you letter.

Sample follow up letter #2

Your name
Street Address, phone, e-mail address

Date

Recruiter's name
Title
Company Name
Address

Dear Mr./Ms./Mrs./Miss …(Last Name):

Thank you very much for the interview and for the information on American Global Relocation Company. I was most impressed with what I learned about your organization.

You did an exceptional job of describing the position of International Customer Service Representative. I feel I could adequately perform those duties with only minimum orientation and training. It is the exciting and challenging job I am looking for.

I am convinced that I can meet the challenges of the job. I also believe that my prior experience with International Finance and Economic Partnership Institute, a travel management company, as well as my overseas living, multicultural experience, and relocation to the USA would prove me well suited for the position.
Working in the field of relocation management with you and your team appeals to me greatly. I look forward to the possibility of the second interview. I will contact you next week to check the status of my application.

Ms._____, thank you for taking the time to meet with me.

Sincerely,
(You can also use "*Yours sincerely*", which is more formal)

Your Name (signature)

Your Name (typed)

Notice in both examples that the words chosen clearly convey the self-confidence and positive attitude of the candidate toward the job.

Follow-up Phone Calls

According to America's leading employment lawyer Jeffrey Allen, "the follow-up telephone call is one of the most important devices in the job search — also one of the most unused". A follow-up phone call is your means to obtain information about the status of the position for which you applied, as well as to keep the employer informed of your enthusiasm for the job.

If you do not hear from the interviewer within one week after the interview, make a follow-up phone call. Try to call at a time when the interviewer is most likely to be in the office. You need to follow up whether or not the interviewer promised to contact you following the interview,

Chapter 6

Here is how you can start the conversation.

"Hello, I am _____ Mr./Miss/Mrs./Ms. _____. I am calling to thank you again for interviewing me for _____ position and to follow up on..."

COMPARISON

Compare: In some countries asking the employer about status of application is rude — not in the US!

If another company has extended you a job offer, call and communicate to the interviewer that you need to know your status in order to make another employment decision.

If you need to speak to the secretary to get to your interviewer, use the following script to compose your message. Practice the call by taping yourself and reviewing how you sound on the phone. Be persistent, but polite, until you are able to speak to the interviewer personally about the status of your application.

This is _____ speaking. May I speak to Ms. Keet please?

If the recruiter is not available and the secretary suggests that he/she takes a message, you say:

Ms. Keet and I met last week regarding the _____position. When is it a good time to call back?

Chapter Summary

Here is a quick review of the follow-up process:

- Follow up with letters/thank-you notes and phone calls.
- Be persistent and polite but not annoying. Keep in mind that there is a fine line between persistence and harassment.
- Practice your follow up call.
- If you have an offer from another company, communicate to the employer that you need to know your status to make another employment decision.

Moving On

After you have followed up your interview with a thank you letter(s) and phone call(s), you have completed all the steps necessary to give yourself the greatest chance of receiving a job offer. Congratulations, your work is almost done. The only thing you can do now is to wait for the offer. In the meantime you should move on the Chapter 7, which describes the sixth and final step in the job search process – finalizing. But before moving on to Chapter 6, reinforce what you have learned in previous chapters by completing the multiple-choice exercise below.

Review of Chapters 1 through 6

To review Chapters 1 through 6, circle the answer that you think is correct. Check your answers against the answer key at the end of the exercise.

1. **The interview is**
    a. A phone conversation between you and the prospective employer to schedule a meeting.
    b. A meeting between you and the prospective employer to assess your suitability for the job.
    c. A meeting between you and the prospective employer to go over your credentials

2. **The interview goal is**
    a. To determine the salary you will be paid
    b. To determine the benefits you will receive.
    c. To persuade the employer that you are the best person for the job

3. **Before you get the job, you need to have**
    a. One interview
    b. Two or more interviews
    c. It depends

4. **You can be interviewed by**
    a. One person at a time
    b. By a group of people
    c. Both

5. **The difference between a traditional and behavioral interview is**
    a. No difference
    b. Traditional interview is old-fashioned
    c. During a behavioral interview you have to perform a task
    d. During behavioral interview you have to quote an example from your past experience

6. **Your portfolio should include**
    a. Copies of your diplomas
    b. Magazine papers related to your profession
    c. Documents and other evidence of your education and experience
    d. All of the above and more if applicable

7. **You should address the recruiter**
    a. Only as Mr., Mrs., Ms., or Dr.
    b. Only by the first name
    c. Unless the recruiter invites you to use his first name, address him as Mr., Mrs., Ms., or Dr.

8. **Choose the correct statement**
    a. Never speak negatively about your past job, country, coworker
    b. If you were very unhappy with your previous job, mention that and explain why

9. **During the interview you should**
   a. Be relaxed and confident
   b. Have a very serious expression on your face
   c. Smile
   d. Be relaxed, confident and smile

10. **During the interview**
    a. Never look into the eyes of the recruiter
    b. Maintain eye contact but do not stare

11. **After the interview**
    a. You should call to follow up on status of your application
    b. You should write the interviewer a thank you letter
    c. Both a & b

Answer Key to Chapter 1 – 6 Review Questions

1–b & c   2–c   3–c   4–c   5–d   6–c   7–c   8–a   9–d   10–b   11–c

Chapter 7

Step 6: Finalizing

In this Chapter: ● Anticipating the offer Negotiating the offer ● Accepting the offer ● Turning down the offer ● Handling rejection ● Things to do after accepting the offer ● Chapter glossary ● Job search process checklist

> *Han ("Harry") Chen, a Canadian citizen, was very happy when he was offered a job with an American Fortune 500 Company. The position he was offered would pay what seemed a good salary (especially taking into consideration the rate of exchange of the American dollar in Canada). The company office was in the heart of New York, Manhattan. It was his dream to work in the US for the leading company in his field and he was very pleased with what he believed to be a good salary. He was confident that he would make enough to provide a good living and, more importantly, to help his mother and two younger sisters. After all, his mother deserved a better life after the hard life in their native China... So, he accepted the offer without any hesitation. He did not even consider negotiating for a higher salary.*
>
> *But when he started looking for an apartment, he was shocked to learn how expensive apartments were in New York. His elation quickly turned to anxiety. Although he had thought his salary was high, he discovered that he would have to work almost three weeks to pay his monthly rent! Furthermore, he needed to pay a large deposit along with the first month's rent when signing the lease. Where would he get such a large sum of money? After all, he had just graduated from college and had no savings.*

What should Harry have done? Was he expected to negotiate? Should he have done some homework before accepting the offer?

In completing Chapters 1 through 6, you have taken the steps necessary to put yourself in the best position possible to be selected for the job. In this chapter, we will discuss finalizing the job search process, including anticipating an offer, accepting the offer, and negotiating the offer. We will also discuss how to deal with rejection of your application.

Anticipating the Offer

Prior to accepting an offer of employment, it is important that you research the salary range associated with the position for which you are interviewing. This will help you make reasonable requests during the negotiation should you be offered the job.

How can you estimate your value in the American job market? The following are some ways to get the information:

- Consult recruitment agencies or search firms
- Search the Internet (try sites like *http://jobsmart.org*, http://jobsmart.org/tools/salary/sal-prof.htm/ and http://www.dbm.com/jobguide/salary.html; www.salary.com)
- Contact professional associations in your field
- Speak to people who work in your field

CAUTION!

Understand that salaries vary depending on the location. *For instance, salaries in the northeastern states may be higher than in the south. At the same time, the cost of living in the Northeast is higher than in the South.*

Negotiating the Offer

Congratulations! Your hard work has finally paid off; you have received a call and a job offer: *"We would like to offer you the position with an annual salary of $XX,XXX."*

NOTE!

As a rule in the US, a job offer will come in the form of a phone call, while a rejection will be in writing.

In previous chapters, we cautioned you to delay all discussions of salary until you receive an offer of employment. Now that you have officially received an offer, it is time to negotiate the offer with the employer. If your new employer has not yet elaborated on the salary and benefits (vacation days, medical benefits, retirement plan, and other "perks"), now is the time to ask him the details of the offer before accepting the position.

Do not let fear of losing the offer stop you from negotiating. Most employers expect you to negotiate, as long as your requests are reasonable.

NOTE!

Most employers expect you to negotiate as long as your requests are reasonable.

Keep in mind that unlike some other countries, in the US negotiating a salary is just one (although perhaps the most critical) aspect of negotiating a job offer.

Before making a final decision and accepting the offer, look at the value of the entire compensation package.

CAUTION!

Be aware of benefits or costs that may not exist in your home country. For instance, the government pays health benefits in many European countries. This is not the case in the US. Be familiar with the cost of living. Keep in mind that certain parts of the US are more expensive than others. For example, the cost of living in New York City is much higher than in most parts of Florida.

Make sure that you confirm the offer: *"Just to confirm, you are offering me the position of (Job Title) at a salary of $XX, XXX?"*

If you feel this salary offer is too low and is not acceptable, you can negotiate the salary. You might say at this point, *"I'm afraid your salary offer is not sufficient to meet my current financial needs. I have obligations and responsibilities that require a minimum salary of $ XX,XXX."*

If the employer values his decision in selecting you as the best candidate for the job, he very likely will come back with another offer that meets your request, if it is reasonable.

On the other hand, it is reasonable to ask the employer for a couple days to think about the offer before you finally accept it. Say: *"I'd like to take a day or two to consider the offer. Is it all right if I get back to you with my final answer on Monday?"*

According to the Society for Human Resource Management, the most negotiable aspect of a new job is the salary, followed by relocation reimbursement and flexible schedule. Health and retirement benefits are generally not negotiable. But ask anyway and you may receive!

NOTE!

Here is a checklist to review while negotiating a job offer in America.

Salary

Find out about salaries in your field. Do they vary based on location?

Does your salary include bonuses? Does it include allowance for working in a specific area?

Are you eligible to earn overtime pay? If yes, how is it calculated?

Benefits

What does the employer offer in terms of:

- Vacation time, sick time. Ask how paid time off can be used. For example, can sick leave be taken to tend for a sick child or spouse? Is there cash reimbursement for unused time?
- Pension or 401K plans
- Stock options
- Insurance (health, life, accident)
- What other perks does the company have? For example, is there: health club membership reimbursement, language lessons for yourself and your family members; will the employer hire a company to help you to find a place to live, to open a bank account, etc.?
- Does the company offer a discount on its products and services?
- Does company provide on-site childcare?

If relocation is required, are relocation expenses/benefits paid? Ask for specifics.

- Will they hire an immigration law firm to secure your and your family's visas or green card?
- Will they provide you a company car or reimburse a rental car? If yes, for how long?
- Will they hire a company to help you and your family to find a place to live, negotiate a lease or find a home to buy, a school for your children, settle in a new location?
- Will they pay for your home leave? If yes, how many times per year?
- Will they pay for your belongings to be shipped to your new job location? If yes, what are the limitations? How much of your belongings are you allowed to ship at no cost to you?

Depending on the type of position and the company's interest to hire you, not all of the points above may be applicable. As a minimum, you should get paid holidays, vacation days, and medical insurance when you are offered a full-time position.

On average the paid annual holiday (it is called vacation) in the US is much shorter than in the majority of the world. The average paid annual vacation in the U.S. is 10-12 days at the time of hire (compared with 30 days in Germany!), but it generally increases with years of service.

STATISTIC

Chapter 7

After you have reviewed the checklist above and have weighed the benefits provided against the salary offered, decide if the salary offered acceptable to you or prepare yourself to negotiate further. Keep in mind that certain items are fixed and others are negotiable. As a rule, salary and other compensation can usually be negotiated, but benefits such as vacation, medical, pension plans, etc., may not be negotiable.

Once you are satisfied and the offer is finalized, ask your employer to summarize the final terms in a letter[6].

Accepting the Offer

After receiving the offer in writing and thinking it over, if it is in agreement with your research and expectations and is acceptable to you, you should call the employer and state your intentions to accept the job. You can say, *"Thank you. I accept your offer. When would you like me to start?"* After notifying the employer of your intention by phone, make sure to follow up your call with a formal letter to confirm your acceptance (see *Things to Do After Accepting the Offer* later in this chapter, and also *Chapter 8, Letters*)

Turning Down the Offer

"Never burn your bridges"
-Unknown-

You may find, after evaluating all the facts, you do not want to accept the offer of employment. If this is the case, reject the offer graciously. Learn how to say "no" politely to your potential employer (See sample rejection letter in *Chapter 8, Letters).*

Handling Rejection

"A setback is a setup for a comeback"
Billy Jolly

"When one door closes, others will open."
-Unknown-

It is inevitable that in your job search you will receive a rejection notice or phone call. Many people experience initial rejection, but eventually, they found the job of their dreams. Never take rejection personally. Do not agonize over it. Keep in mind that it is a competitive market. It is just a business decision. Of course it hurts. But never feel like you are "damaged goods." These setbacks do not reflect negatively on the character of the job applicant, but rather on job requirements. Remember that when one door closes, others will open.

NOTE!
Understand that rejection is a part of the process.

Although you may have difficulty or fail at first – it will all come together if you keep trying.

---

[6] We do not use the word "contract" in the US. Instead "offer letter" is used because it is not legally binding.

TIP FOR SUCCESS!

When you receive a rejection, always ask if the employer knows of any companies that may need people with your qualifications and skills.

When you receive a rejection letter or phone call:

- Remember that, as a rule, it takes several interviews to get a job offer.
- Evaluate the reasons why you did not get the offer.
- Do not let the rejection depress you.
- Learn from this experience so that next time, you are more successful.

TIP FOR SUCCESS!

*Learn from experience, and move on. One of the most important values of American culture is reaching goals and being successful by **learning from mistakes**.*

Things to Do After Accepting the Offer

You have officially accepted the job offer. What now?

Do not relax yet! Continue creating a positive impression by writing a letter to your new boss. (See a sample acceptance letter in *Chapter 8, Letters*). Express your enthusiasm about your anticipated responsibilities.

Do not forget to thank those who helped you throughout your search: people who gave you references, as well as those who gave you advice during your networking. Tell them about the job you have landed and how grateful you are for their help and support. (See a sample letter in *Chapter 8, Letters*). Offer your own help and assistance should they ever need it. Remember, they are part of your network.

Further Resources and Literature

www.Monster.com – the site lists salary information for different professions, industries and states

www.salary.com and **www.salaryexpertt.com** – same as the above.

Hampshire, David. *Living and Working in America*. London, England: Survival Books, 2002, p.297

Graber, Steven. *The Everything Get A Job Book*. Holbrook, MA. Adams Media Corporation, 2000

Chapman, Jack. *How to make $1000 a minute negotiating salaries and raises.*. Ten Speed Press, 1987

Messner, Max. *Job Hunting for Dummies*. New York, NY: IDG Books Worldwide, pp. 317-326. – more detailed information on benefits

Chapter Review

Let's review the important points of Chapter 7.

1. Most employers anticipate that you might negotiate as long as you are reasonable.
2. Find out the going rate for the salaries in your industry and the prospective job location.
3. Understand cost of living in the area you are moving to.
4. Before accepting the job offer, look at the entire value of the package.

5. Make sure to get a letter of confirmation of the employment offer.

6. Write acceptance letter.

7. Turn down the offer graciously.

8. Do not let rejection depress you. Learn from the experience and move on.

Chapter Glossary

Allowance: additional payment

Benefits: paid programs including but not limited to paid vacation days and medical insurance

Bonus: an extra payment typically paid quarterly, semi-annually, or annually

Compensation: payment, salary

Credentials: qualifications

En route or resettlement expenses: expenses (typically meals and transportation from and to an airport) while traveling from origin location to destination

Insurance: coverage can include medical, life, accident, and disability

401K plan: a retirement savings plan managed by an employer. (Employees contribute to 401K plans and the company matches a part of those contributions. All 401K plans have tax advantages).

Layoff: termination of employment

Overtime: Pay on top of the salary when work is performed outside normal hours or on weekends (required by law for certain types of employees)

Pension plan: compensation you will receive from the company when you retire (this is becoming less common in the US)

Perks: extras provided by the employers, e.g., discounted membership, tuition refund, employee discounts on company stock, etc.

Reimbursement: refund

Relocation: moving from one country or location to another

Retirement plan: pension plan

Severance pay: money paid if company terminates employment, lays you off.

Shipping company: moving company, removal company

Stock options: when company gives the employee the right to buy or sell company stock at a specified price within a certain time frame. This can be offered as a bonus, part of compensation.

Temporary living: living in a hotel or temporary housing before moving into a house or an apartment

Travel expenses: airfare, train tickets, mileage, lodging and meals

Job Search Process Checklist

BEFORE THE INTERVIEW

 Research the Company

 Products and Services

 CEOs

 Lingo (industry-related vocabulary)

 Culture

 Prepare a list of common interview questions and answers

 Prepare your own questions

 Rehearse (videotape, critique)

 Prepare your portfolio

 Find out the directions to interview, visit the location beforehand

DURING THE INTERVIEW

 Arrive ahead of time

 Know the general interview structure (be ready for the small talk)

 Listen, make eye contact

 Ask the questions you prepared in advance

 Check off your questions

 Keep your answers to the interviewer's questions targeted and focused

AFTER THE INTERVIEW

 Follow up with a thank you letter

 Make follow up calls

AFTER THE JOB OFFER

 Negotiate the offer

 Accept or reject the offer with a formal letter

Chapter 8

SUCCESSFUL JOB SEARCH TOOL BOX

In this Chapter: ● Communication tool box ● Self-presentation. ● Working the room ● Networking phone conversation ● American table etiquette ● Accent reduction ● Portfolio ● Letters ● Technology-based communication tools ● Phone skills in the job search●Using e-mail in the job search

<table>
<tr>
<td rowspan="3">Job Search
Toolbox</td>
<td>1. Social tools
Self-presentation.
Working the room
Networking phone conversation
American table etiquette
Accent reduction</td>
</tr>
<tr>
<td>2. Material Tools
Portfolio
Letters</td>
</tr>
<tr>
<td>3. Technology-based tools
Job search related phone skills basics
Using e-mail in the job search</td>
</tr>
</table>

Communication toolbox

Effective communication is the key to a successful job search. You may have the best educational credentials and excellent qualifications. However, in the US job search culture, if you cannot effectively communicate your abilities and professionalism both in business and social settings, you will not be able to compete successfully. To compete successfully in the US job market, you need to be armed with a number of communication tools.

In the course of the book, you were introduced to a number of the basic tools designed to help you get the job you want. This Chapter contains additional information on those tools as well as some additional tools to apply to your job search. The toolbox consists of three "compartments": *social tools, material tools* and *technology-based tools*.

Under social tools we will cover self-presentation, working the room, ability to hold a networking conversation, American table etiquette and accent reduction. The second group contains material tools. These include the professional portfolio and several types of letters. And finally, technology-based tools, are phone skill basics and e-mail skills to apply to your job search.

We will start with how to introduce yourself (self-presentation), then move to how to handle yourself at social and professional gatherings. This will be followed by how to showcase your accomplishments by putting together a portfolio. You will find samples of letters that will help you to reinforce your professional image. And eventually you will learn how to communicate effectively via technology.

Additionally, you can learn about building your business vocabulary and accent reduction tips in *Ameri$peak* (see Resources and Literature after this Chapter or check out the information on www.SucceedinAmerica.com).

Social Tools

Self-presentation

Self-presentation is describing yourself to the others in a few words.

At any meeting, event or gathering, you are presented with numerous opportunities to meet people who can help you with your job search. Therefore, it is important to be able to connect with them. The connection process begins with a self-presentation, in which you introduce yourself to each of these contacts one-on-one. In your introduction you should state your name clearly and provide your listener with a *concise* statement of relevant information about you. For example:

> *My name is Nara Venditti.*
>
> *I am a career coach. I help individuals become more effective in looking for a job, changing careers, improving interpersonal skills, and moving up in their organizations.*

According to an American expert in socializing, Susan RoAne, what you say specifically about yourself should be tailored to the situation and the nature of the gathering you are attending. If you are attending a professional association meeting, you would state what job you do or what you are educated to do (as I have shown in the example above). On the other hand, if you attending a birthday party, your profession is not as important as your relationship with the hosts. In this situation, a more appropriate introduction would be:

> *Hi, my name is Janet. I am Ellen's sister–in-law.*

Whether you are introducing yourself professionally or socially, always keep your introductions short, upbeat, and relevant.

TIP FOR SUCCESS!

Make your self-presentation short and upbeat.
Use relevant information about yourself; tailor the self-presentation to the event.
Use action verbs. Douglas Richardson, in his book on networking says "action verbs get you remembered. Passive don't." (See more about action verbs in Chapter 2, Action Verbs)

In job searching, it is a good idea to develop and rehearse two variations of your self-presentation, a professional one to be used at the interview and another for social occasions.

Here are a few more examples of introductions I might use for myself in a business-related environment:

- *My name is Nara Venditti.*
  I work for myself. My company name is Succeed in America.
- *I am an educator and speaker. I do seminars and speak at the events.I help individuals and organizations with such issues as communication in the workplace, customer service, workplace based ESL, employability and cultural understanding.*
- *I am a writer. I wrote two books, one on how to get a job in the United States and another on American Business English.*

In most situations, I would use only one or two parts of this self-presentation (depending on the event and who I am talking to).

Chapter 8

Here are two more examples of business related self-presentations.

1. *Hi, my name is Erika. I am a secretary. I help businesses to run efficiently and smoothly. I type, file and answer the phones.*

2. *Hello! My name is Edgar. I am an interpreter. I help people and businesses to communicate with each other.*

COMPARE
Compare business self-presentation with a self-presentation at a social event (wedding). "Hi, my name is Judy. I am the sister of the bride."

Self-presentation Worksheet

To create your own self-presentation, fill in the blanks in the exercise below. Use my example further down to help you create your own self-presentation.

1. Greeting/Your name: *Hi! I am* _____ *(My name is*_____*).*
    Example: *Hi! I am Nara Venditti (My name is Nara Venditti).*

2. What your qualifications are: *I am*
    _____
    Example: *I am a career coach.*

3. The importance of what you do and how it may be beneficial to the others:
    _____
    Example: *I help immigrants and foreign-born to get employed, become better communicators and move up in their organization.*

Once you fill out this worksheet, you will have a draft of your self-presentation.

Actions to take: Develop and rehearse variations of self-presentations for:
1. Social occasions (a party, a birthday)
2. Job interviews
3. Semi-formal gatherings (club meeting, company picnic)
4. Networking phone conversations
5. Business meetings (meetings with clients, association meeting)

To deliver an effective self-presentation, use this preparation checklist:
1. **Write out** several ways to describe who you are and what you do.
2. **Check with a native English speaker** to be sure that your word usage is correct and sounds natural.
3. **Practice your self-presentations** over and over again until you can express them smoothly and with confidence.

One good way to practice any oral presentation is to record it on tape it and then play it back so that you can listen to yourself. Do you speak clearly? Is your accent so strong that others might have difficulty understanding you? Do you sound confident? sincere? comfortable? Finally, do you understand what you are saying?? (Don't laugh. This has happened to me many times when I have used this technique to evaluate my own speeches, and wondered what I was really trying to say!) Try improving your presentation and record it again. Keep trying until you have perfected your presentation. You can also practice in front of a mirror, in the car, or with a friend.

TIP FOR SUCCESS!

1. *Use action verbs when introducing yourself. Refer back to the action verb list in Chapter 2. For instance: "I am an architect and I design resorts" or "I am a photographer and I take creative wedding pictures."*

2. *When you introduce yourself, remember to smile and maintain eye contact with the other person.*

Your contact may introduce you to others, refer you to someone who may know about job openings, give feedback on your resume, or suggest organizations to join or courses to take. Don't be discouraged, however, if the first person you approach is not receptive. Politely move on to the next person. Whatever advice or help your contacts offer, make sure to thank them for their time and effort. Be sure to reciprocate when they need help. (See a sample of a simple thank-you note in the Exploratory Interview section of Chapter 4.)

Now that you have your self-presentation ready, it is time to use it in networking at business and social events.

Working the Room

> *"Talk to anyone about himself and he will listen without interrupting."*
> Herbert V. Prochnov

> *"The aim of small talk is to make people comfortable - to put them at their ease...*
>
> *It's a game, like tennis, in which the object is to keep the ball in the air for as long as possible."*
> Michael Korda

Have you ever been to a party, wedding, or reception where you were too shy to speak to people? Perhaps you were shy because you were not sure what words to choose? Perhaps you felt uncomfortable because nobody approached you and you didn't know how to approach others? If you answered "yes" to these questions, do not despair. Meeting people and carrying on a conversation is not only an art; it is also a science and it can be learned.

How to Start a Conversation

Imagine you are at a party or reception. What do you say to start a conversation? How do you approach people you do not know? What questions are appropriate to ask? What topics are appropriate to discuss? How do you "work the room"?

In the US, start a conversation with a general, non-business-related comment – this is called "small talk."

Small talk is a "warm up" or prelude to that part of the conversation in which you will seek answers to your job-search related questions. The aim of small talk is to connect with people, make them comfortable and to like you.

COMPARE

Remember that appropriate and inappropriate topics vary across cultures. In the US, avoid discussing another person's income or financial situation, religion, politics, or any controversial topics. Do not go into deep discussions of a topic, but change topics often to maintain superficial and light discussion. Good topics to discuss are weekend and vacation plans, theater and movie shows, the weather, work, cars, pets and sports.

Chapter 8

COMPARE

There is a difference between making light conversation over the phone and talking in person while at an event. When calling someone on the phone promptly ask "how are you?" or say "good day/evening";, then identify yourself and ask for permission to continue: "Is this a good time to talk?"). If the individual is receptive, explain why you called.

A telephone call rarely presents the opportunity to develop a relationship or bond with the listener. (For more information, see "Networking Phone Conversation" later in this chapter.)

According to Herbert Prochnov and other experts, small talk in the US is like tossing a ball from one person to another. Do not keep that ball too long. Allow the opportunity for the other person to speak as well!

TIP FOR SUCCESS!

To be introduced to other people, it is a good idea to come to the event with an American friend or someone who is comfortable in American social settings.

TIP FOR SUCCESS!

If you are very new to this country or new at networking, go to events to learn how to network. Watch other people interact with each other. Work on memorizing and practicing their body language, words, pronunciation and intonation until you can do it comfortably on your own.

Not everyone is naturally good at small talk. Some people have difficulty initiating and carrying on small talk simply because they do not know what to say or are unsure of appropriate topics. Others have difficulty expressing themselves in English. Fortunately however, it is easy to develop this useful skill once you learn and practice the rules of small talk, the American way!

NOTE!

Not all Americans are adept at "small talk, American style", so learning how to do it will put you "ahead of the game" (which means "will give you an advantage")

CAUTION!

Remember this: Never come up to a person and say "Hi my name is_____ and I am looking for a job."

To review, here are the important steps to follow and practice at gatherings in order to wok the room and become comfortable interacting with others.

- Initiate the conversation
- Transition to a small talk
- Maintain a conversation by asking and answering questions.

The following is the formula on how to initiate a conversation. I called it the"4S Formula".

1. The easiest opening gesture is a smile, so remember to **SMILE** and make eye contact.
2. Extend your hand for a hand **SHAKE**.
3. **SAY** "Hello. My name is… And your name is?"
4. **SAY** "Nice to meet you!" or "It is good to meet you!"

Next, transition to small talk. Here are a few approaches:

1. Ask *"How did you get involved with the International Institute?"* or *"How do you know the hosts of the party?"* or *"What a wonderful garden the hosts have!"*
2. Ask *"What type of work do you do?"*, *"What do you do?"* (Meaning "what do you do for a living?"), or *"What is your profession?"*
3. You may also discuss the weather (*"It is so nice outside! Do you know what it will be like tomorrow?"*), a new movie, latest news, or talk about the event (*"What brings you here?"* or *"Isn't this a great event?"*)

Here are some tips to maintain the conversation.

1. Keep the conversation light and short.
2. Maintain a friendly smile.
3. Say the other person's name a couple of times.
4. Show interest in and connect with the other person by asking questions that allow the person to talk about herself/himself. This is important because, as a rule, Americans enjoy talking about themselves and welcome multiple questions.
5. Change topics often but stick with appropriate topics such as sports, pets, weather, travel plans, hobbies, movies, and your or the other person's occupation.

COMPARE

Unlike many other cultures, if you are the person starting a conversation, it is okay to extend your hand first (regardless of your age, gender or social position).

So, start a conversation with small talk. If you are from another country, beware of inappropriate topics.

CAUTION!

1. Never go into detail about your health or personal misfortunes. 2. Never ask how much money people make. 3. Do not talk in depth about politics.

TIP FOR SUCCESS!

If you do not know the person, start with "Hi, my name is _____. What is your name?" Try to remember the person's name. One effective way to remember the name is branding. For instance, if somebody's name is Rose, associate the person with the flower.

Ask questions or make statements inviting the person to continue conversation. Here are some examples:

- What is your hobby?
- Where are you from originally?
- What do you do for living?
- Have you read about _____ in today's paper?
- Jack wanted me to say hello for him.
- Doesn't our hostess look gorgeous today!
- Isn't the food great?
- Don't they have a beautiful house?
- Isn't the weather wonderful/awful today?
- What do you do when you are not working?
- How do you know Elena?
- I know the host - we are neighbors (or: we work together)
- Do you have children? (be careful about this question; if they do not have children you may make them uncomfortable)
- Are you a California native? (Are you a Chicago native?)

Chapter 8

- What brought you to this event?

Ask questions to get the other person to talk about himself. Tell stories and try to relate them to the subject of conversation. Use humor if you are good at it, but be aware that appropriate humor may differ across cultures.

CAUTION!

When telling jokes, keep in mind that humor is perceived differently across cultures! What is funny in one culture may be offensive in the other. For instance, in some countries sarcastic humor is acceptable. It is not always the case in the United States!

COMPARE

Appropriate and inappropriate topics for small talk vary across countries and cultures. For instance, you can engage Armenians for hours in conversation about politics and they will be impressed that you are knowledgeable about Armenian culture and history. At the same time you should avoid topics about politics with Americans unless they initiate the conversation.

The following paragraphs present a few more ideas, tips, and strategies on how you can carry on a conversation and feel comfortable interacting with those around you.

Establishing a Connection
(Attracting the Other Person's Attention, Find Something in Common)

Always apply three "C's" when you are engaged in small talk: connect, connect and connect. Here are some ways to establish a connection with someone that you do not know well:

- Mention things you have in common: places you have been to, hobbies you have, mutual acquaintances, etc.
- Call the other person by name a couple of times during the conversation. Use the other person's name when departing company. Say "Good-bye, Tony, it was nice meeting you."
- Be a good listener. Do not monopolize the conversation or talk about yourself too much. Express interest in the other person and his or her comments and views.
- Remember that in the US small talk is like tossing a ball back and forth. Ask a question, let the other person talk, and then ask another question or let the other person ask you a question. In other words, take turns speaking!
- If for some reason you wish to postpone speaking to someone, politely ask for a business card and an opportunity to contact the person later: "Do you have a business card? Perhaps we could chat later?"

Things Not to Do

Do not discuss salaries or how much another person makes unless the other person brings it up. In the US, asking a person about income or salary is considered very rude.

Avoid political discussions unless you detect an interest from the other person. Politics is not an accepted introductory or business topic in the US.

Do not spend all of your time with the people you know. Acknowledge them with brief hello but steer yourself toward others who you wish to meet. For example, you might say to your friend "Hello John. It's nice to see you here. Excuse me, I see someone I'd like to meet. I'll speak to you later."

Do not interrupt when someone is speaking to you. Wait for a pause in the conversation before you interject.

95

Politely Ending the Conversation

When you wish to end a conversation, do it politely — finalize your thought or wait until the other person finalizes his or hers. Wait for a pause and end with a friendly good-bye by saying something like one of these examples:

> *Excuse me, I want to catch Russell before he leaves. It was good talking to you.*
> *Excuse me. I'd like to get something to drink. It was great meeting you.*
> *Excuse me, I'd like to say hello to my old friend before she leaves. It was nice seeing you again.*

More Things to Do

- Treat the networking event like a party and enjoy mingling with people. All you need to do is to meet a future friend or two who can introduce you to other people, or maybe you will meet someone who will influence your life in a very positive way.
- Remember that you need to meet new people at the event to nurture your network and to get closer to your goal.
- Follow up after the event: call the people you've met or write them notes.
- If the person responds, acknowledge by sending another e-mail or note or calling again. Then contact the person in a week. If the person responds again, you've made a friend who can become a part of your network.
- Include the person's name in your contact list and e-mail in your "address book". Email or call that person from time to time. Send him/her holiday and birthday cards.

You have now learned the basics of savvy socializing, which you can apply to your job-search-related business interactions – as well as your personal interactions during networking events. It is time now to use your knowledge at real events.

Networking Phone Conversation

Business communication using the telephone is a widespread practice in the US. This includes networking over the phone. To increase your opportunities for making contacts in your job quest, you should learn how to converse with people over the phone, which differs from face-to-face conversation. In this section, we point out the elements of a well-structured networking call, provide examples of conversation to illustrate the approach, offer a worksheet to help you develop your own personalized networking call, and take you through a role play to practice your call.

Effective phone networking conversations generally have six distinct parts:

1. **Greeting/Your name.** Hello! I am [your name]
2. **Connector phrase.** Tell where you met previously met or who referred you.
3. **Ask for permission** to continue the conversation. For instance, "Is this a good time to talk?"
4. **Self-presentation.** Concisely state your qualifications and indicate why you called.
5. **Ask for information.**
6. **Close with a "thank you".**

Let's take a look at this example of a good networking phone conversation, which follows the six-part outline:

1. *Hello (Hi) Mr./Mrs./Ms. Johnes, my name is Mico Farada.*
2. *I was referred to you by Rick Delgado. (See other connector phrases listed below).*
3. *Is this a good time for you to speak? (or: Do you have a couple of minutes? Do you have a moment to speak with me now? Did I interrupt anything?)*
   Note: If this time is not acceptable, ask: *When is a good time for me to call you?* and skip to Part 6.

If this time is acceptable, continue with Part 4.

4. *Rick told me that you might know about an opening in the research department for somebody with my skills and experience. (or: Rick told me that you are a good person to talk about the IT field.) I have extensive experience in the area of rubber research.*
5. *May I forward you my resume? May I follow up at a later date?*
6. *Thank you for taking the time to talk to me.*

Before closing any conversation, **do not forget to thank** the person for his or her time and effort to help you.

Connector phrases are phrases that establish a connection or common ground with a person you are networking with. They help the other person to feel comfortable and at ease with you.

TIP FOR SUCCESS!

Make sure to use connector phrases before you start a conversation with a new contact.

Some more examples of connector phrases are:

- I am new in this country and I could use some help in getting oriented.
- We met at the wedding party.
- Jane Licardi suggested that I call you. She and I worked together for two years at XYZ Company.
- I attended your presentation, and it has transformed my life.
- Your speech was very thought provoking and educational.
- I was told that you are a leading expert in this area.
- We are members of the same organization.
- I am considering making a transition, and I was told that you could point me in the right direction.

Now that you know the proper structure of a networking call, use the worksheet below as a template to prepare your own call.

Networking Phone Conversation Worksheet

1. **Greeting**. Hello! My name is

_____

2. **Connector Phrase**

_____

(e.g. James Logan suggested that I call you).

3. **Asking permission.** Is now a convenient time for you? (Do you have a minute right now?)
   If yes, go to point 4 and 5
   If no, ask: *When would be a good time to call you?* (Follow up at a proper time).

4. **Self-presentation.** *For the past five years I have been working as*

_____

Then add: *I have [extensive] training [experience] in* _____ *and I am looking for a position in the* _____ _field*

5. Asking for information.
Do you know of a business or organization that would be interested in employing somebody like me?

6. Thank the other person.

Note: You can modify this worksheet to create one for in-person conversations or networking letters.

Here are two further examples of the effective networking phone call.

1. *"Hi, my name is Elena. Your colleague, Bob Aldrich, told me to call you. Bob told me that you own a fitness center. I have ten years of experience teaching aerobics. I am looking for a business or organization that can employ somebody like me. May I drop by and talk about this with you in more detail? [Alternative: Do you know anybody in this field whom I may contact?]*

2. *"Hello, may I speak with Mr. Jones please? Good morning, Mr. Jones, my name is Fabiana. I was speaking with your colleague, Vanessa Ricardi, last week. She suggested that I speak with you about potential job openings in your department. Is now a good time for you? Or, should we schedule an appointment or a phone conversation at a more convenient time?"*

Role Plays

To reinforce what you learned and practice your networking skills, conduct some role-playing exercises. Find someone to "role play" with you.

Sample outlines

1. You are calling a contact that you met at a party.

   - Introduce yourself.
   - Remind the person where and when you previously met .
   - Ask for permission to continue the conversation.
   - Tell what you can do (use your self-introduction).
   - Say what you would like the other person to do.
   - Thank the other person.
2. You are attending the party or gathering (specify what type of event it is)

   - Use your short self-presentation (appropriate to the occasion)
   - Use your opening question
   - Discuss some topic or talk about the event you are attending
   - Politely end the conversation.

Further Resources and Literature:

Brown, Dale. *Learning for Living*. Woodbine House Inc., US, 2000.
Lilian Glass, Ph.D. *Say it Right. How To Talk In Any Social Situation*. Harper Collins Publishers, Inc., 1990.
Mackay, Harvey. *Dig Your Well Before You're Thirsty*. The only networking book you'll ever need. New York, 1997
Encyclopedia of Associations published by Gale Research - contains the list of national and international organizations listed by field and alphabetically.
RoAne, Susan. *How to Work a Room (learn the strategies of savvy socializing - for business and personal success)*. Shapolsky Publishers, New York, NY, 1988.

Chapter 8

Richardson., Douglas B. *Networking*. John Wiley & Sons, 1994
Volunteer! The Comprehensive Guide To Voluntary Service In The US And Abroad.
www.VolunteerMatch.org – Website for volunteer opportunity for "whatever you like doing" in the U.S.
www.idealist.org – A directory of non-profits all over the world. Browser will find organizations by mission statement, topic or geographical location.
www.nonprofitexpert.com – When you select "Resource Links" from the menu on this Website, you will find an extensive list of links to non-profit organizations around the globe.

American Table Etiquette

Interviews over a meal are quite common in the US. If you are invited to a meal interview you need to apply American table etiquette in order to project a professional image. Keep in mind that table etiquette varies from country to country. It may vary by:

- table manners
- layout and use of the utensils used
- serving order of different courses
- the way the food is served
- how people interact during the meal
- the food itself.

Before going on a meal interview, it will help you to review and become aware of the following American customs pertaining to table/meal etiquette:

The Interviewer's Gender

Here are guidelines to follow if your interviewer is of the opposite gender.

Situation #1: Your interviewer is a woman and you are a man. Be polite but not gallant. For instance, in many countries a man is expected to help a woman to her chair (Poland, Russia), but in the US a professional woman is independent — she will not expect you to help her to her chair or into her coat.

COMPARE

In some cultures males are expected to be dominant and gallant. Not in the US! As a nation, Americans are committed to equal rights for women. For this reason, women are expected to be treated as equals to men.

Situation #2: Your interviewer is a man and you are a woman. Expect your interviewer to be friendly and professional and treat you as an equal, not as a representative of the opposite "weak and beautiful" gender. Do not expect your coat to be held and do not flirt.

What to Order?

Think about appropriate foods to order *before* getting to the interview. Here are some tips:

- Have an idea beforehand what meal you will order. This will allow you to chose a meal quickly without wasting time looking at the menu. Employers sometimes view such hesitancy and uncertainty as a reflection of one's inability to make a timely business decision.
- When ordering, choose a meal in the mid-price range of the menu. This suggests you have sensible taste, i.e., you are neither cheap nor extravagant.
- Choose a meal that doesn't require a lot of your attention. For instance, don't order a whole lobster or chicken Kiev because they are too messy to eat. You certainly don't want to splash lobster juice or the hot butter of the chicken Kiev all over your clothes or, worse, your interviewer's clothes.

Alcohol/Smoking

Alcohol and smoking are considered inappropriate at interviews in the US. Never order an alcoholic drink; Americans ban alcohol in the workplace or in other professional situations, especially with unfamiliar associates.

Do not smoke, even if you are in a designated smoking area. American society as a whole opposes smoking. For this reason, disclosing that you are a smoker can work against you in the hiring process. Many believe that employees who smoke tend to take more breaks, be less productive and get sick more often than employees who do not smoke.

Napkin

Spread the napkin on your lap.

In some countries the table etiquette dictates keeping the napkin on the side of the plate or tucked into one's collar. In the US it is customary to spread the napkin on your lap.

COMPARE

Order of Serving

"They served me coffee at the beginning of the meal - does it mean they want me to leave!?" If you are Italian, you may think that being served coffee at the beginning of the meal is an invitation to leave. In many parts of Italy, coffee is served at the very end of an occasion and guests leave shortly after. The order in which the food is served in the US may be different than that in your country. In the States, drinks come first, then appetizers, salad and soup, followed by entrées (main course) and dessert. Coffee and tea may be served at any time during the meal.

Silverware and Glasses

You may be intimidated by the amount of silverware on the table. Always remember the simple rule: use it from the outside in. For instance, if you have two forks, use the outside one for your salad and the inner one for your dessert. Generally, Americans use a fork to eat cake (Compare: spoons are used for the same purpose in Russia and Armenia).

Remember the simple rule: use silverware from the outside in.

NOTE

Most right-handed people hold a fork in their right hand. If you need to cut your food, switch the fork to the left and cut with the right hand. Then switch the fork back to your right hand to continue eating.

Eating with the fork in the left hand – as is done in many parts of the world – is also acceptable and may be considered fancy and sophisticated.

However, if your culture dictates not to use silverware at all or use it in a limited fashion (e.g. Ethiopia) it is advisable that you follow the American custom. Absolutely do not soil your fingers by using them instead a fork or spoon.

In the US, it is customary that your drink (be it water, soda or iced tea) is on your right. Do not pick up your future boss's glass, which will be on your left!!

NOTE

Chapter 8

How to Interact During the Meal

Follow these basic rules when interacting with others during the meal.

- Do not begin eating before your interviewer. However, if you are the last to be served you should say "Don't wait, please start".

- Participate in the conversation during the meal. However, do not dominate the conversation. Let others do most of the talking.

Do not speak with food in your mouth! Spitting food at your interviewer is as bad as splashing.

CAUTION!

Never complain about the food or service! Be pleasant throughout the meal; remember, as a guest you have to be gracious.

Who Pays the Bill? (Or as we say in the US, "Who picks up the tab"?)

Generally, the person extending the invitation (in this case your potential employer) pays the bill in full. By the way, you do not have to reciprocate the invitation.

Saying Thank You

Be sure to thank the interviewer after the meal, and do not forget to thank her/him again in your follow-up note.

Further resources and literature:

Baldridge, Leticia. *News for new times*. Scribner, NY, 2003.
Forni, P.M. Choosing Civility. *The Twenty-Five Rules of Considerate Conduct*. New York. St. Martin's Press, 2002.
Fox, Sue. *Etiquette for Dummies*. Wiley Publishing, Inc., NY, 1999.
Wanning, Esther. *Culture Shock! USA. A guide to customs and etiquette*. Portland, Oregon: Graphic Arts Center, 2000, pp. 95-100.

Accent Reduction

What is an accent? Simply put, an accent is the combination of pronunciation and intonation. Varying degrees of these two factors result in a variety of different accents.

Pronunciation is the result of such factors as the positioning of the vocal cords, tongue and lips as well as the amount of stress and the duration of sounds while speaking a language. Intonation is the melody, rhythm, and speed of speech. Different languages have different sets of sounds and different melodies of the speech. They also vary by average speed.

When you speak English, your accent depends on your base language. If your base language is lacking some sounds that the English language has, you might have particular difficulty pronouncing those sounds. For example, it may be challenging for native speakers of Russian to pronounce the [H] sound. Native speakers of Spanish and Arabic may have difficulty in pronouncing the sound for [V]. As a rule they would pronounce [B] instead. By the same token, Koreans would pronounce [L] instead of [R], since the [R] sound is non-existent in Korean.

Be proud of your heritage and your accent but, at the same time, be aware that an accent can impact your ability to communicate and, consequently, affect your ability to achieve your goals. If your speech cannot be understood by those in a position to hire you, promote you, increase your salary, or become your family or friends, then the doors to opportunity may be closed to you. You may ask, "Is it realistically possible to eliminate my accent?" If you came to the US as an adult, eliminating your accent altogether may be impossible. That's the bad news (as they say in America). But do not despair! The good news is – it is not at all necessary to eliminate an accent altogether. While a heavy accent makes it difficult to understand your speech, a light accent can work to your advantage as long as others understand what you are saying. Let me explain this.

While Americans tend to have difficulty understanding foreigners with heavy accents, a light accent that does not distract from the clarity of speech is often considered charming and, for certain jobs, can even be a desirable quality in a job candidate. For example, an American company that markets products internationally may realize increased sales through a salesperson who can communicate clearly yet still retain his/her native accent. In this case, the accent has a subtle appeal that can work to establish a rapport (or connection) between the company and the client. Therefore, taking steps to reduce, but not necessarily eliminate, your accent can help you in your job quest.

There are several ways to go about reducing your accent. You can purchase or borrow from your local library an audio or video guide aimed at accent reduction. You can hire either a language pathologist or accent reduction coach. Or you can do what I did: work on your accent reduction yourself using the following tips that proved effective for me. Some of the tips will also help to expand your vocabulary.

- **Listen to American speech and try to emulate American accent.** If you are in the US, you have the advantage of immersion into a live language. In addition to watching movies and listening to TV and radio programs, you can engage yourself in live communication with Americans, anywhere and anytime – for example, at your workplace, the supermarket, and even at the Department of Motor Vehicles.
- **Join Toastmasters**. One of the best ways to mix with Americans and improve your speaking in public is to join a Toastmasters Club. You can find a Toastmasters Club in virtually anywhere. Just go to www.toastmasters.org and look for a club close to you. When you visit or join a club, ask the club members to jot down the words in your speech they did not understand. Practice saying these words at home and incorporate them into your speech at the next meeting.
- **Tape your speech.** Analyze the tapes and jot down frequent mistakes you make. Ask for feedback from others. Create a list of most frequently mispronounced words, expressions and constructions. Work on the list daily; read the units over and over again until you get them right.
- **Read aloud every day.** While you read, tape yourself. Listen to the tapes. Repeat words over and over. Remember, minimizing an accent takes practice.
- **Tape real-life conversations.** Create your own list of the most frequent words and expressions. Pronounce them over and over again until you get them right.
- **Buy or borrow from your local library an audio and a printed version of the same book.** Listen to the audio while following the text. Try to repeat sentences and tape yourself.
- **Listen to the media.** Listen to American reporters speak. They speak standard American English.
- **Borrow tapes from the library.** Make this enjoyable. Listen to the kind of tapes you enjoy most. Do it while you are driving, walking, performing home chores. If you enjoy the book, the time will go by fast and you will have a chance to improve your listening skills and vocabulary as well as work on reducing your accent.
- **Speak slowly and enunciate.** Enunciating means pronouncing the sounds very distinctly. Pay special attention to the endings and vowels.

Chapter 8

- **Be persistent.** It is a lot of work, but your efforts will be rewarded. Change does not happen overnight, but it does happen if you are positive and persistent. Remember, persistence is one of the underlying values of the American culture!

Some Resources and Literature

Accent Reduction Made Easy. Penton Overseas. Abridged edition, January 1, 2003
Cook, Ann. *American Accent Training.* Barron's. Matrix Press: USA, 2000.
Hope, Donna. *American English Pronunciation: It's No Good Unless You're Understood* (Books 1-3). Cold Wind Press; Bk & Cassett edition, 1999
www.accurateenglish.com – accent reduction training
www.toastmasters.org – A non-profit organization developing public speaking and leadership skills. Find out about a club in your area either on the web or by calling (949) 858-8255.

Material Tools

Portfolio

> *"One picture is worth a thousand words."*
> Unknown

Are you an articulate speaker in your native language, yet you have difficulty in presenting your work and describing your accomplishments in English? If so, why not let your work speak for itself through a *portfolio*. A portfolio is a collection of evidence of your qualifications and experience. A portfolio can include, for example, your resume, samples of your work, articles you have written, public news articles written about you and your work, and audio or video tapes of your public appearances. Your portfolio showcases your professional skills and provides tangible proof of your competence. Consider putting a portfolio together.

TIP FOR SUCCESS!

A well organized, professionally prepared portfolio can be a powerful tool in winning a job.

Each job application may require presentation of different portions of your portfolio. For example, if you apply for a mechanical engineering position, your portfolio should include blueprints or photographs of the equipment or projects you were involved with. Be ready to explain the items that you present. For instance, *"This is a photograph of the most recent high-speed linear scanner that I and my colleagues designed."*

Now that you know what a portfolio is, it is time to create one.

Follow this easy checklist:

- Decide on your portfolio contents
- Collect the materials
- Prior to each interview, decide which components of your portfolio are relevant to the particular job
- Rehearse your presentation of your portfolio. For instance, say *"In this picture you can see a building I designed two years ago"*; or *"This video tape represents my presentation on nuclear physics at the international conference"*.

You may wish to prepare your portfolio in hardcopy form or as an electronic file. Or you may wish to have both.

Hardcopy version. To organize your portfolio in hardcopy form, follow these steps:

- Put together individual pages. Apply the samples and photos of your work onto cardboard and laminate them. Alternatively, place your samples in plastic sheet protectors. These work well especially for certificates.

- Fasten the sheets into a ring binder.

Electronic Version. If possible create an electronic version of your portfolio. It has a couple of advantages over hardcopy. First, if you have access to a computer and know how to create your own website, you can effectively market your skills by displaying your portfolio on-line. Most Internet service providers offer free space to build a website. Geocities.com is one site that provides instructions and space to create a free website. Secondly, if you ask and receive permission to bring your own laptop to the job interview, you can present your portfolio electronically. You can even conveniently leave a CD copy of your portfolio with the interviewer.

Letters

Letters are another important communication tool when seeking a job in the US. There are several major types of letters that you should be familiar with:

- Response to an advertised position –written in response to a classified ad or position opening announcement (see sample in *Chapter 2, Cover Letter*)
- Notification to an executive recruiter – written to inform an executive recruiter that you are available (see sample in *Chapter 3, Executive Search Firms*)
- Follow up/thank-you letter –sent to your interviewer after a phone or face-to-face interview (see sample in *Chapter 6, Follow-Up/Thank You Letters*).
- Networking interview thank-you letter – written to people who took time to help you network (see sample in this chapter)
- Letter for accepting a job offer – written to the job offer or to confirm your acceptance of a job (see sample in this chapter)
- Letter for declining a job offer – written to the job offer or to politely decline a job offer (see sample in this chapter)
- General thank-you letter – written to people who helped you in various ways during your job search (see sample in this chapter)

The following are examples of the last four letter types in our list:

Networking Interview Thank You Letter

> *January 24, 2007*
>
> *Juan Santana*
> *55 Mill Drive*
> *Stalley, New York*
> *Attn.: Tom Paraskevides*
> *All-American Gadget Company*
> *American City, State XX00X*
>
> *Dear Tom:*
>
> *I greatly appreciate your taking the time to meet with me today. The information I received is invaluable in my quest to learn more about diversity in business and the industry in general.*

I will read the materials you gave me and explore the websites you referred me to.

I am looking forward to attending the event on January 30th and will follow up with you on the particulars in a few days.

Truly yours,
Juan Santana
Juan Santana

Letter Accepting an Offer

December 14, 2007

Peter Italiano
55 Mill Drive
New York, New York

Americo Recruiter
All-American Company
Uscity, State, USA

Dear Mr. Recruiter:

Thank you for offering me the opportunity to work at All-American Company. I am very happy to accept the position of accounting analyst with your financial department. The position entails the kind of work I have always wanted to do, and I am confident that I will do an excellent job. I can't wait to begin.

Please let me know if there is anything I can do to facilitate the transition to my new job.

Thanks again.

Sincerely,
Peter Italiano
Peter Italiano

Letter Declining an Offer

December 14, 2005

Peter Italiano
55 Mill Drive
New York, New York

Americo Recruiter
All-American Company
Uscity, State, USA

Dear Mr. Recruiter:

I spent two days considering your offer of Marketing Associate with All-American Company. After evaluating all aspects of the offer and my own situation, I concluded that it will not be the right move for me under the present circumstances.

I appreciate your offer, but I must decline.

I wish you all the best in your future endeavors.

Sincerely,

Peter Italiano

Peter Italiano

Thank You for Helping Letter

December 14, 2007

Peter Italiano
55 Mill Drive
New York, New York

Ms. Connie Contact
All-American Company
Uscity, State, USA

Dear Ms. Contact:

I would like to inform you that I have successfully concluded my job search. Starting next week, I am beginning my new job as an operations manager with Unitech Inc. This position is exactly what I was looking for and provides me with ample opportunity to grow.

The professional advice, contacts and recommendations from you ensured my success.

Thanks for helping. If there is anything I can do for you in the future, please do not hesitate to ask.

Sincerely,

Peter Italiano

Peter Italiano

Further Resources and Literature:

Eyler, David R. *Job interviews that mean business.* New York, Random House, 1999.
Krannich, Caryl Rae, Krannich, Ron. *201 Dynamite Job Search Letters (5th Edition),* 2004.

Technology-Based Tools

The US is one of the most, if not the most, technologically developed country in the world. Americans use technology extensively in communication. For this reason, job-related communication skills, over the phone and via e-mail, are important.

Chapter 8

We talked about some aspects of communicating over the phone in previous chapters. In the sections that follow, we will talk more about phone and e-mail skills as they relate to your job search in the US. Also, you can find guidelines on technology-based communication in the resources listed after each section.

Phone Skills in the Job Search

Handling the phone well speaks to your overall professionalism. When looking for a job in the US, there are several situations you should be aware of. As in many countries, the telephone in the US is an important means of business communication. Voice mail (typically an answering machine that accepts the call and allows the caller to leave a message) is much more popular in the US than in the rest of the world. With some phone answering systems, the candidate can push "0" to get a live person if he/she doesn't want to leave a message on the machine.

COMPARE

The popularity of technological communication has dramatically increased throughout the world. However, use of voicemail in many parts of the world either is nonexistent or is not widespread. By the same token, voice mail in the US is a popular business communication tool. For this reason you need to use it properly and professionally.

In the following paragraphs we discuss the most common telephone communication situations affecting your job search and suggest guidelines for making the most out of telephone communications.

1. Creating a Professional Phone Greeting (Recording)

Create a professional phone greeting (the recorded phone message on your own answering machine). An employer will call you if your resume has impressed him and he wishes to invite you for a face-to-face interview or a phone interview. (See Chapter 4, *Tips on Phone Interviews.*) Your voice message has the power of making or breaking that first impression when your potential employer calls you. Make sure that your phone greeting is designed properly. Tape it over and over again to ensure that it is clear and professional. Keep in mind that your message should be short, informative and to the point. If it is longer than about 30 seconds, there is a chance that Americans will lose patience and delete it before they hear the entire message.

CAUTION!

If you are not at home and your voice mail or answering machine message is not clear and is not phrased properly and professionally, chances are the caller will not even leave a message.

Here are some samples of simple voice messages: *(Begin your message with a professional greeting such as "hello" ("hi" is also acceptable) and end with a "thank you" closing.)*

Sample 1
Hello. You have reached Gabriella. Please leave a message and I will call you back as soon as possible. Thank you.

Sample 2
Hello! This is Mazy Ping. Please leave a message and I will call you back as soon as possible. Thank you.

Sample 3
Hello. You have reached Vasumati and Sriram Rao's residence. Please leave a message so that we can return your call. Thank you.

Sample 4
Hello. This is Manfred Dieter. I am on vacation until July 16 and will not be checking messages until I return. Please leave a message and I will call you back on my return. Thank you.

2. Answering a Recruiter's Call Live

Most often you will receive a recruiter's call on your home telephone. Therefore you should develop a simple greeting that is appropriate for all your incoming calls, and use it to greet both personal and business callers.

> Say: *"Hello, this is [Your Name] speaking."* or *"Hello, this is [Your Name]"* or, *"[your name], speaking"*
> Example: *"Hello, this is Joanne speaking."* or *"Hello, this is Joanne.",* or *"Joanne speaking".*

3. Returning the Recruiter's Call

If a recruiter has left you a voice message, return the call as soon as possible (within 24 hours). When you call the recruiter back, your call will not likely be answered directly by the recruiter himself. Most often it will be received by either an automated voice message or by a company telephone operator, receptionist or secretary. Follow these tips in order to be prepared for all situations:

- Before you call, compose your message and write it down. (Use the script outline below to compose your message and remember to keep it short.)
- Read it aloud and edit the script until is sounds correct.
- When you are ready, call the recruiter.
- If you are connected to the recruiter's voice mail, read your script to the answering machine when you are prompted to leave a message. When leaving your voice message, make sure there is no background noise.
- If a person answers your call, always give your name first. (Identifying yourself at the onset of the conversation speaks to your professionalism). Then request to speak to the recruiter. For example, you can say one of the following:
    > *"Hello, this is [your name]. I'm returning Mr. Delmark's call. Is he available?"*
    > *"Hello, this is [your name]. May I speak to Mr. Delmark please?"*
    > *"Hello, this is [your name]. I'd like to speak to Mr. Delmark please."*
    > Upon being connected to the recruiter, identify yourself again and explain that you are returning his call.

Use the following outline for composing your message if you have to call the recruiter back:

- **Your name, who you are and when you called** (This is Myra Roberts. It is 5 p.m, on Tuesday, October 29)
- **The reason why you are calling**
    - o I am calling in response to your message...
    - o I am calling to set up a meeting (an appointment, an interview).
    - o I am calling you in response to an advertisement... to set up an interview.
    - o I am calling to follow up on the interview of last week.
    - o I am returning your call regarding scheduling an interview.
- **Leave your number** (speak slowly and distinctly and repeat the number twice). Please call me at (203) 791-1107. I am looking forward to your call. Thank you.

TIP FOR SUCCESS!
When leaving a message on somebody's answering machine, mention your phone number twice. Say it at the beginning and then repeat at the end of your message: "Again, my number is..." By repeating the number you will increase the chances that the employer will return your call.

Remember to keep your message short, informative and to the point (about 30 seconds) so that the caller does not lose patience with your message.

Chapter 8

Further Resources and Literature:

Fisher, Judith E.. *Telephone Skills At Work*, McGraw-Hill Companies, The Crisp Pubns., Inc., 1993

Friedman, Nancy J. *Telephone Skills from A to Z: The Telephone "Doctor" Phone Book,* Crisp Pubns., Inc., 2000

Morey, Doc. *Phone Power: Increase Your Effectiveness Every Time You're on the Phone*, Random House, Incorporated, 1999

Powerful Telephone skills. National Press Publications, Rockhurst College, Continuing Education Center, Career Press, Nawthorne, NJ 07507, 1993.

Smith, Debra A. *Professional Telephone Skills, Vol. 2,* CareerTrack Inc, 1995

Using E-mail in the Job Search

E-mail is used more commonly in the US than in many other countries. US companies rely heavily on e-mail communication. Generally speaking, e-mail messages are less formal than conventional, written communication. However, when sending an e-mail to a recruiter you should be somewhat more formal in your style and follow the format of a business letter. In this section we outline some basic guidelines for writing job-search-related e-mail messages.

E-mail message structure. Like any other communication, an e-mail consists of three major parts: 1. introduction, 2. the body of the message, 3. the closing. In addition, e-mail has a subject line, which comes first. Make your subject line self-explanatory so that it is very clear what your message is about. It should be specific and as brief as possible (five words or less). *For example: Translation Job Application, Service Industry Convention Schedule.* By providing a short, self-explanatory subject line you will ensure that your message will not be deleted before it is read. Let's illustrate a typical e-mail communication:

Subject line: State subject in one to five words. Example: *Audit Position Application.*

Introduction: The introduction consists of two parts, the salutation and connector phrases.
1. Salutation:
   Dear Mr..... or *Good morning, Ms....*
   Make sure to spell your recipient's name correctly. For example, if your recipient's name is *Mr. Browne* (spelled with "e" at the end), make sure you do not address him as *Mr. Brown.*
2. Connector phrases -
   Thank you for your advice... Hope you are keeping warm in New England winter... I am e-mailing you to follow up on... As we discussed... Per my voice mail...

Body of Message: Describe why you are writing.
   I wanted you to be aware of my most recent paper presented yesterday at the International Conference on Nuclear Physics. It was voted the best technical paper in the proceedings, and it is directly applicable to the work your company is doing on the Alpha Project. My paper can be accessed via the Conference website. Here is the web address www............com. I hope you will consider this work in addition to the other works in my portfolio.

Closing: The closing normally consists of two parts:
1. Discussion of the next steps and specific timeframes.
   I will follow up on the status of my job application in two days.
2. An expression of thanks and concluding thoughts.
   Thank you for your consideration. I am looking forward to hearing from you again.

Signature:

End the email with *Kind regards, ...Regards, ...*or *Sincerely, ...* followed by your signature or AutoSignature complete with contact information (your name, phone number or numbers, e-mail address). For example:

Kind regards,
Nick Valenti
(203) 791-1107
nv@SucceedinAmerica.com

Do's and Don'ts for a Business E-mail

Do	Don't
• Use informative subject line • Use spell check • Proof read • Have someone read your e-mail before you send it to the recruiter • Use simple sentences • Use short paragraphs • Use bulleted phrases • Use spaces and paragraphs	• Include graphics with your auto signature. The company's firewall might not let it through. • Use abbreviations, jargon, slang, acronyms • Use internet speak punctuation, e.g. lol,): (which means laughing out loud") • Use lengthy sentences • Capitalize words whenever unnecessary • Use attachments

Further Resources and Literature:

Ameri$peak (the most common words and phrases you need to know to communicate effectively in American business). Succeed in America, 2006

Angell, David. *Elements of E-Mail Style: Communicate Effectively via Electronic Mail.* Brent Heslop (Author), Addison-Wesley, 1994

Flynn, Nancy, Flynn, Tom. *Writing Effective E-Mail: Improving Your Electronic Communication.* Crisp Pubns., Inc., 2002

Booher, Dianna. *E Writing: 21st Century Tools for Effective Communication* . Simon & Schuster Adult Publishing Group, 2001

Chase, Maureen, Trupp, Sandy. *Office Emails that Really Click* by Aegis Publishing Group, Ltd., 2000

CONCLUSION

Now you that you know how the job search process works in the US and have the tools, knowledge and resources, it is easier to get the job you want in this country.

After you have read this book, I encourage you to supplement your learning by seeking more in-depth information and exploring the resources listed at the end of each section. Also, go to the local library or bookstore and look at the books in the *Jobs, Careers* and *Business Communication* sections. Read about American culture and language. Sign up for courses in business communication.

It is now time to integrate your knowledge and skills in your job search!

Be positive, confident, and proactive and you will achieve your goals and dreams! Your success is my success!

Dr. Nara Venditti

If you have thoughts, comments or ideas about this book, I'd love to hear from you. This is the first edition and if you found a mistake or misprint or have any comments, please e-mail us at nv@SucceedinAmerica.com.

You can find the latest updates to this book on my website and in my newsletter *Succeed in America*. To subscribe to the newsletter, e-mail me at nara@SucceedinAmerica.com.

My website address is http://www.SucceedinAmerica.com.

Ameri$peak

A mini-dictionary of the most common words and phrases you need to know to communicate effectively in American business

On the pages of this glossary you will find a list of the key words and expressions you need to know in order to be comfortable talking to and understanding people in an American business setting. This knowledge is essential to anyone who works in the USA, aspires to work here, or works with Americans abroad. Learning the vocabulary in this book will enable the non-native speaker of English to become a better, more confident and equipped communicator in American business.

This dictionary offers the following benefits, and more!
- helps you to communicate confidently and effectively in American business
- provides you with the right amount of key words and expressions needed for daily business interactions with Americans and others proficient in English
- helps you to create your own customized business vocabulary.

Here is what business is saying about Ameri$peak

"I wish I had this [dictionary] several years ago, when I was trying to find my way in the business/professional world, where the use of idioms is so wide spread, there is hardly a sentence it is missing from ...I'm sure this will be very handy to any one who is not too familiar to American English.
Eli Ben-Ezra, Senior Sales Engineer, NextNine Inc., Israeli national, USA

"This is a very interesting concept and I believe this will prove popular in many countries. I do have people working for me in the UK whose first language is not English. They would benefit from understanding and using these phrases. ...you [Nara Venditti] have created something unique that can add significant value to many people around the world.
Simon Morris, Director, Global Marketing, ClickSoftware (NasdaqSC: CKSW), UK

As an immigrant from Hong Kong, I spent my first months in this country watching TV commercials to "get into the culture". Similarly, I had to spend a tremendous amount of time listening to folks at work, especially during meetings, to learn the essence of American English. I am sure new immigrants will find your dictionary extremely helpful as they enter the business world. Great job!
Catherine Bui, Director of Customer Support, PeopleSoft USA, native of Hong Kong SAR, China

"As a leader, I have learned the lesson and value of open, honest, and credible communication. And, as an individual responsible for organizations around the world, I am very sensitive to and appreciate the difficult factors involved in effective global communications. As hard as we may try to eliminate acronyms, slang, and business phrases from our international communication, they are an inevitable part of our language. This publication will go a long way to help non-native English speakers understand some of the nuances of the English language. I think it should also be required reading for individuals with global communication responsibilities as a reminder of the flagrant use (and abuse) of such phrases."
Richard Guenther, Vice President and General Manager, Maintenance Support Services, Unisys Global Infrastructure Services, USA

This book is available from your local bookseller, online supplier,
www.SucceedinAmerica.com *or by using the order form on the last page*

112

About The Author

Dr. Nara Venditti is the president and founder of *Succeed in America!*, a consulting firm that helps individuals and organizations with such issues as workplace-based English language skills, career counseling, employability, customer service, cultural understanding, relocating spouse adjustment and employment. Dr. Venditti is recognized by the State of Connecticut as a naturalized US citizen who made contributions to better the lives of refugees and immigrants in this country.

Over the past 25 years she held positions ranging from an educator to in-house international assignment consultant.

Author of 61 published works, she is a third-generation educator and the recipient of a State of Connecticut official citation for her tireless dedication to making a difference in the community.

Throughout her 25-year career, she has been working with adult learners in both academic and business environments. Dr. Venditti is an adjunct lecturer at Western Connecticut State University, columnist in ethnic and business periodicals and a host of Channel 23's Community Forum Public Television Program.

Succeed in America!, LLC
offers customized workshops for your organization.

Here is what the participants are saying:

"(Nara's) sense of humor is nicely integrated into her speeches... it drives home points and keeps the audience involved and listening."
Association For Service Management International Convention, Seminar Participant, Reno, Nevada, USA
E-mail nv@SucceedinAmerica.com or Call (203) 733-6068 or (203) 791-1107
www.SucceedinAmerica.com
See workshop descriptions and more testimonials on the next page.